Under the Hood

Also by the Author

Under the Hat

Under the Bed

Available from www.bookguild.co.uk

Under
the
Hood

What's under there? Let's find out

Linda Porter

The Book Guild Ltd

First published in Great Britain in 2015

Second Edition published in Great Britain in 2018 by
The Book Guild Ltd
9 Priory Business Park
Wistow Road, Kibworth
Leicestershire, LE8 0RX
Freephone: 0800 999 2982
www.bookguild.co.uk
Email: info@bookguild.co.uk
Twitter: @bookguild

Typesetting in Garamond by Ellipsis Digital Ltd, Glasgow

Printed and bound in Great Britain by CPI Group (UK) Ltd, Croydon, CR0 4YY

ISBN 978 1910298 350

British Library Cataloguing in Publication Data.
A catalogue record for this book is available from the British Library.

For my children, who taught me so much

Acknowledgements

I would like to give many thanks to Sue Leet for supporting and nurturing this project during its birthing stage, also to Greg Forde for pushing me in a very person-centred way from the beginning of the journey that culminated in the writing of this book, and to all my great friends, clients and colleagues, for sharing your experiences, which by doing so you have helped to spread the word.

Contents

Introduction

I was ten years old when my grandfather told me a story about his time in Germany during the Second World War. Suddenly a bus was careering out of control down a hill towards him. He managed to move quickly out of the way, but saw the bus slam into a young woman. 'It was as if all the life came out of her body – it started at her head and went all the way through her, down to her feet and out. I saw it, I saw it move through her body, I will never forget her face.' I remember listening, fascinated, but saying nothing. 'Come on, it's lunchtime,' he said, and in we went. He never spoke of it again and neither did I, and it was from that time that I realised I was able to listen to a story and not only remember it, but also to 'carry it' or file it away in some sort of interesting, often enthralling inner place.

I wrote this book because my clients told me I should, and being a good therapist I always listen to my clients. There are four main stories: The Grandmother's Story, The Mother's Story, The Father's Story and The Daughter's Story; all of them are true. Told to me through the years since childhood, they show us a psychological history of how behaviours and attitudes can be handed down, and about a mysterious force at work called unconscious attraction.

Sometimes a child can be born into a family with a very different personality or make-up to the other family members. During my work as a therapist, many of the clients who come to me with their story will say they feel like the black sheep of the family. They feel they are different from the other family members; they struggle to relate and to feel they belong. Sometimes they feel that it's so marked, they wonder if they've been adopted. Very often we find their problem family is actually an emotionally unhealthy family and because the client is a different personality, they are unable to enter into this unhealthy way of relating and living life. One client put it rather well: 'There are more black sheep than white, and it's the white sheep who have all the problems.'

What can happen is that the 'black sheep' goes forward, resolving to do things differently and an unhealthy pattern can finally be broken.

Ever since I was a small child I always loved to hear people's stories. Did I become a therapist because I was told these stories and loved to hear them, or was I told these stories because I was a budding natural therapist? All I know is it's the right place for me to be and I love my work.

I can remember various family members telling me stories through the years about their childhoods and their lives. 'Tell me again that one about... !' was a common cry. Nowadays, when listening to client's stories, I need to concentrate acutely, as one missed sentence could mean that an answer they are seeking is lost. To be able to sit with a client while they tell their story, to be able to accept anything they tell me, and to hear repetition without becoming bored or impatient is something that has always come naturally to me.

People come to see me for all sorts of reasons: relationship problems, anxiety, depression, bullying, domestic violence, stress and abuse are just some of the issues that drive people to seek help. I only need one incident in the story to tell me about a person, and then we can start to answer the questions. The question everyone comes with is 'Why?'

'Why did he abuse me?' 'Why did she leave me?' 'Why am I so anxious?' 'Why aren't I happy?' 'Why did she do that?' 'Why can't he talk to me?' 'I keep crying, why?' The list could go on. The Cognitive Analytical Therapy (CAT) that I work with uses the psychology of behaviour to explain these kinds of questions. Often there are several possible answers and the client will pick the one they feel makes sense to them; after all, they are the ones with first-hand knowledge of their situation so they know best which explanation fits. Once they have an answer, their way of thinking can change in regard to what their problem was. They can then go forward in a new way, with new techniques for living life.

Every client has a story to tell; it's part of their healing. Clients' stories consist of snippets and glimpses of times remembered; sudden switching of events, little cameos of isolated incidents, like the story my granddad told me. There is no background setting of scenes, no preparation of characters, no formal beginnings and often no end. As a therapist, I am not there to ask questions for my own enjoyment or satisfaction.

Clients' stories can be interesting, exciting, intriguing, passionate, full of anger, very sad, tragic or sometimes even boring. I may need to ask them to give more detail if we are trying to discover an answer to a question, but the important thing is their need to tell their story and I am there to listen, ready to pick up anything significant that will assist me in giving the help they are seeking. A friend once said, 'Surely you don't remember all your client's stories!' Not consciously of course, but if a part of a story or an incident is mentioned, then it all comes flooding back, as has been the case with certain clients returning in a current crisis after many years.

The stories in this book are told very much in the way that clients give their stories to me: little snippets and glimpses over the years, chunks of life handed down. As we can follow the story through three generations, we have the advantage of knowing some outcomes, but more importantly we get to recognise how each generation affects the next and how behaviour can sometimes be learned and handed down. We see the different personalities and how the theory of attraction works.

'Under the hood' in the American sense means under the bonnet where all the inner mechanisms that allow a car to perform (or not) are working away, but we can't see them without lifting the hood and looking at what's going on.

'Under the hood' in the English sense means under the hood of a jacket, a 'hoodie', concealing a part of the person, so the more the hood is pulled up and over the face the less of the person we can see. The family in these stories often have their hoods pulled up, or their car hoods kept down, so no one including themselves will need to see or acknowledge what's really going on, and like the hood of a car, if we ignore what's underneath for long enough it will be to our detriment and sometimes our peril.

This is a social history with ways of life that have disappeared, also a psychological history showing behaviour patterns – and maybe more importantly, tools for change in the toolbox which most of the family members never had. So let's go under the hood to find out what's really going on, and to answer that common question: 'Why?'

The Grandmother's Story (Ellen)

A Suffolk Childhood

I was born at the turn of the century, not long before Queen Victoria died. My mother and father worked in London at the Queen's Head Hotel in Putney; my father as bar manager, my mother as a servant. There was already my sister Grace, and it was becoming very impractical by the time I arrived as my parents 'lived in', which meant they had one room in the hotel, now with two babies as well. My father, loving the social atmosphere of bar work, eventually found an alternative to suit us all – or so he thought. A pub called the East India Arms in the heart of the City of London required a live-in manager and it wasn't far from where my father had been brought up. On four floors with fantastic views across London (now of course dwarfed by office blocks) it was perfect for his growing family. Today, the East India Arms is a still a City workers' pub, closed at weekends when the area is more or less deserted. In my father's time it was the banks and Stock Exchange that provided most of the 'City gents' clientele. My father (who I called Dadda) loved it; he was responsible for the whole building with a live-in domestic servant to clean and cook. He had his two loves, his work and his family, under one roof.

We hadn't been there long when my mother (Mamma), decided things were not as they should be. Women were not seen in pubs in those days – well, that's what Mamma used to say. Definitely not the place to be bringing up children, and Mamma was from the country, which meant she knew about these things, or so she said. Dadda on the other hand was brought up in London, his parents running another City pub in the nearby Fleet Street area. As children, he and his sisters, sitting on the back stairs, would watch the constant stream of people: banker's clerks and office boys, shopkeepers and barrow boys. Sometimes he would run errands for them, earning himself a penny or two. Dadda said the East India Arms provided very good money, and where would they find such free accommodation in a little country town like Sudbury, where Mamma came from? It was the work Dadda had always known, he was a true Londoner born and bred, and he did not want to leave. What was to be done? They couldn't agree, and finally Mamma packed us up, took us back to Sudbury, and moved in with her sister. So me and my sister Gracie were brought up in Sudbury with Mamma, while Dadda continued to live and work at the East India Arms, sending money to Mamma, and this is how it always was for us as children.

Many years later, when he was seventy-five, he became ill. I brought him home to me, and looked after him until he died a few months later.

As children, we never questioned the fact that our parents never lived together. It was a situation we had always known. We were not aware of any bad feeling, I always remember they were very civil to each other, but it wasn't long before Gracie and I were old enough to travel by ourselves to see our father, Mamma putting us on the train to London, and Dadda meeting us at the other end at Liverpool Street station. They never met again as far as we knew, so probably neither forgave the other for wanting what they felt was right.

One of my earliest memories with Mamma was when I was about four years old, and I realised that children played in the street – but we didn't. 'Don't talk to the children in the street, Ellen! They're rough.' To me they weren't rough, but were children just like we were, with their street games. Some had no shoes, but we weren't well off either. Later it was 'You can't play in the street, Ellen, it's not nice.' Mamma was brought up above her father's butcher's shop, her mother was a dressmaker, her sister had been a servant like herself, and her brother was an errand boy, but certain standards were important to my mother. I remember the census man coming to the door and she made a great thing of the fact that under 'occupation' she wanted him to write 'private means' so it could be seen she had money and was not living in her sister's house because she was poor with nowhere else to go. She couldn't talk to people easily; no wonder she hadn't liked the rawness of London. Mamma had gone to London at sixteen because a lot of young women did. You could easily get jobs in service, as a servant in a household or a hotel and the money and living standards were much better than in the country. Sudbury had one silk factory where if you were lucky you could get a job; otherwise it was mostly seasonal work on the land.

Maybe she'd had dreams of Dadda managing a hotel, similar to where they were living when I was born, something that to her would be more comfortable and with more status and 'niceness' than a London City pub.

Visiting Dadda in the school holidays, we would walk through the City from Liverpool Street station, seeing lots of men (who we called 'City gents') looking very smart in suits and bowler hats, past grand buildings, to the pub. He was always pleased to see us and we loved it as it seemed very exciting to walk through the bar full of these City gents, and creep under the lift-up counter top to climb the iron spiral staircase that ran up the middle of the building.

As well as beer, hot Oxo was served at the bar, and I can remember sitting on the stairs watching with fascination the extremely long-handled spoons being used to stir the Oxo drinks in the very tall glasses. I still have one of these spoons, used all my life, very useful for getting the remains from the bottom of jars and bottles. Sometimes we would be taken for a ride on a horse bus or take the electric Tube to visit Dadda's family. I remember saying to Mamma after one of these long visits, 'It seems quite posh, with those City gents,' but all Mamma would say was that it had been 'the best thing' to be in Sudbury.

Dadda was lovely to us, very affectionate, my mother being rather withdrawn. I have a framed photograph he sent me when he joined the Freemasons, looking splendid in his regalia and underneath he has written 'with best love from your Dad.' This is quite in contrast to other family photos and writings of that time which were very formal; not expressive as this was.

Living with Mamma's sister, our Aunty Em, we had no bathroom and an outside toilet – but that was normal then. Aunty Em had a husband, Uncle Fred, and there were cousins Fred and Jack and eventually little Kate, who I stayed very close to all my life. They were just like real brothers and sisters, as we were brought up with them almost right from when we were babies. Our little family: me, Gracie and Mamma, had one bedroom and our aunty and uncle with our cousins had the other bedroom and that was normal too, parents and children together.

In those days, Sunday school played quite a big part in our lives. It must have been a marvellous way for the grown-ups to have a break from the children, as there were two Sunday school classes a day and we had to attend both. Nothing to do with the family's idea of religion; I don't remember any of the adults ever going to church.

Every Sunday all of us children would walk to the Sunday school, about two miles there and back each time. Before starting this walk we had to go in the opposite direction to a farm, to get milk for the family. It was skimmed milk which I now understand would have been cheaper than full fat milk, although unwittingly more healthy for the adults and probably not meeting the requirements for growing children. Grace, Kate and myself would set out for Sunday school in our 'best dresses'; we had one other dress to wear on weekdays called a 'sailor suit'. After having dinner at home, our walk would be repeated for the afternoon Sunday school. We must have walked at least six miles on Sundays, with the farm and two Sunday school trips, but I don't remember minding. There were no cars so we were used to walking everywhere, and Sunday school was fun with the other children. Remember we had no TV or radio, so it kept us occupied for the whole of the day.

There was one thing I remember that I really didn't like and that was in the day school. We had to lie for periods of time on the floor on a wooden board. This was supposed to make our backs grow straight, for which we also had to wear a boned bodice underneath our sailor suits, to keep our shoulders back. It was all very uncomfortable and the board and floor were very hard. Oh, the longing to be able to move around, to be able to go out and play in the sunshine! But no, we all had to lie on our boards on the floor for what seemed like such a very long time. I have no idea how long a time it actually was. Our childhood energy made this all so frustrating and difficult, but we did it; we obeyed without question. But maybe it did prove to be effective as now people remark on my straight back.

Very few people had holidays away that I knew of. Sometimes Gracie, Kate and I would be taken to Hunstanton in North Norfolk, where one of Mamma's brothers now managed a large hotel, so we didn't have to pay a lot of money to stay there. It was seen as a very long way to go and our friends thought we were very lucky.

At home on Sundays and Mondays, there were cakes for tea, and the rest of the week we had bread and 'dripping': the solidified fat left behind from the meat cooking. It could be spread like butter, and was very tasty but this time not healthy for the adults!

Monday was 'washday' all day long, so our dinner was packed up in a basket to be taken to school: sandwiches and a home-made bun. There were no school dinners then. Coming home to dinner on the other school days meant more long walks. School was just over a mile away so it must have meant that most weekdays, with coming home to dinner, we were walking four miles a day. I managed to get the little job of carrying the books home for teacher to mark. Her house was on my way and I was always a helpful little thing. For this I would get a ha'penny (pronounced 'haypny'). Sometimes the teacher would let me leave school early to go to her grandfather's cottage where I would make his tea and toast. I liked these little jobs, leaving the schoolhouse behind with everyone still there was like an adventure, and the grandfather was always pleased to see me. He would say 'Hello, little Ellen!' and tell me stories. Another time I was allowed to leave early was when I had a piano lesson. We were lucky, as not every family could afford to pay for these. It was only for me and Gracie though, so it must have been because of Dadda's money.

On Saturdays we were given a farthing each (a quarter of a penny) and this would buy us a stick of liquorice, or a home-made toffee wrapped in newspaper. Sometimes we saved the farthing so the next week we had a ha'penny and that got us a big stick of twisted toffee called 'honeysuckle twist'.

Eventually I left school at thirteen, and because I always liked sewing, I got an apprenticeship at a dressmaker and draper's in Sudbury. The hours were 8.30 a.m. – 5 p.m. Monday to Saturday, with half an hour for lunch. There were no wages paid during this apprenticeship, which lasted two years.

When the apprenticeship ended I bought a bottle of port wine and cakes all round, as this was the expected traditional celebration. I was now starting work 'properly', earning one shilling and six-pence per week. The hours were even longer now, 7.30 a.m. until 5.30 p.m., still with the half hour for lunch, and no tea or coffee breaks. The 'well-off people' as we called them would have dresses made in the spring and there were orders for wedding dresses and bridesmaids' dresses too. I was hand-sewing and there would be alterations to do as well, but this situation was not going to last for long.

Changes

During the last few years, Mamma had been ill and was gradually get-ting worse; she was coughing a lot and short of breath. It was lucky we were living in our big family as there were not so many demands on her. Suddenly Mamma died. She was forty-two. Gracie and I found we were leaving the family. Dadda was arranging for us to go and live with our aunts, his two sisters, in London. It meant we would be near Dadda which we were really looking forward to, but it was very hard leaving the family we had grown up in, waving goodbye at the station to a tearful little Kate, promising to visit when we could.

Neither Aunty Evie nor Aunty Jessie were married and the family called them 'the spinster aunts'. We thought they were very old, although they must have been only in their fifties. They were kind however, and would get our breakfast for us before we travelled on the Tube to work. I managed to get a job at Marshall and Snelgrove, a big department store in Oxford Street. The working hours were better in London: 9 a.m. to 5.30 a.m. and a half day on Saturday too. There were two weeks' holiday a year, and we would save two shillings a week on a card towards it. Two of the girls went to Canvey Island and we all thought this was wonderful. I would go back to Sudbury to see my family. All the working day, I was making handmade blouses with about twenty other girls and a very strict forewoman in charge. No talking was allowed and if she went out of the room it was suddenly bedlam as we all made the most of it with our chatter! At 1 p.m. she would line us all up in twos and march us down to the canteen. Sometimes we had the foreman, who was kind and sympathetic to us. We all liked him and called him 'Father'. I used to get hungry during the mornings; after all, breakfast with the aunts was at 7.00 a.m. and there was no morning break, so I would secrete food under my work table. I managed to get away with this for a few months, but one day the horrible forewoman caught me, and gave me the sack! Everyone sympathised, including Father, and one of the girls walked out with me. It was a time of lots of work in London and so it wasn't very drastic, we got new jobs straight away. Unfortunately, we only managed another few weeks as there was another horrible forewoman!

Eventually I ended up at a company called Benjamin's in Golden Square: two tiny houses knocked together to make one, and it was drab, dark and dirty. Piece work on handmade blouses meant taking work home as well, partly to earn as much money as you could, but also to do what they expected of you, and I did not find it a happy time. However, by now the war was on and Dadda arranged for us to move to Kingston, a bit further out of London, away from the City and the West End, where his brother and family lived and although the aunts had been kind, it was lovely to be in a lively family again. There was Uncle Edward and Aunt Lizzie, our cousins Ed and Lily, and also Nellie, another cousin who I subsequently stayed close to all my life. We would catch the train to Waterloo and go on the sixpenny 'drain' (Waterloo and City line) or sometimes walk across Hungerford Bridge to work, and my work didn't seem so bad now.

Then something else happened. Gracie had not been well, having had a cough for a long time and it was starting to be feared she had the same TB that had killed our Mamma. Dadda arranged for her to go away for a while to Ventnor on the Isle of Wight to a special sanatorium and she also went for a few weeks to Hunstanton for the cleaner air. One day when I got off the train at Kingston station after finishing work, I saw Dadda and Uncle Edward coming to meet me. They brought me the sad news that Gracie had died that afternoon in the garden. She was nineteen years old.

During the following weeks, Nellie was a comfort. We talked about Gracie a lot, and I cried and cried. Nellie had a boyfriend, John, who was away fighting in the Great War, as all the young men were. One day John came home on leave bringing a friend with him, George. George came from Sudbury too, and John thought it might cheer me up. It was just what I needed. I knew of his family as his father ran a big building business in Sudbury, and I had vague memories of him at school, but what was most important, he made me laugh. We started to go out.

George had lost his mother when he was fifteen; the same age I had been when I lost Mamma. He told me how his father had married again straight away, a young girl not much older than George himself. Grieving his mother and angry with his father he had run away from home, lied about his age and joined the army. He was now caught up in the Great War. He vowed never to speak to his father again. There was also a rift with his younger brother, and he was sad at leaving his little sister.

There was a war on and no one knew whether they would live or die, so when George asked me to marry him I said yes. We married quickly in Sudbury. None of his family came, but my father came down from London, and we had my cousins and friends. John was best man and Nellie was my bridesmaid. Married for a year and living back in Sudbury, I realised I had made a mistake. I made my life in my four children. George and I were married for nearly fifty years.

Under The Hood Part 1

Mamma and Dadda's Relationship

One of the reasons the relationship broke down between Ellen's parents was because Dadda and Mamma wanted different things. Wanting different things can be a prime cause of a relationship eventually ending. This situation is a good example of how a relationship changes when children are born. How are we going to approach parenthood? Hopefully we will be compatible in our ways and expectations. Both parents working in service meant sharing a way of life, with a common goal. Once the situation changed and there were babies to think about, the goal unfortunately was not a shared one. Coming from two different backgrounds didn't help, as attitudes and expectations can vary. Dadda, brought up in the heart of London, not understanding why the children can't live there – after all, he had. Ellen thinks they probably never forgave each other for wanting what each felt was right, and anger can be a common result when each partner is unable to meet the needs of the other. This could explain their complete cut-off from each other once the children became a certain age and were able to travel on the train by themselves; but also they were very different personalities, as we shall explore.

They both had their sense of responsibility and were caring towards the children. Dadda was 'always pleased to see us' and they visited regularly, through to adulthood and beyond. He sent money home up until Mamma died, when he arranged for his girls to live in London, and paid for them too. His ability to show affection is apparent with the warm writing on the formal photograph, and Ellen's lifelong relationship with him, eventually bringing him to her home to nurse him when he was dying. Mamma on the other hand is described as withdrawn, not talking to people easily, and we don't hear anything else about her apart from her need for certain standards. It is difficult for a child to become close to a parent who is withdrawn, as closeness comes from the adult responding to and reaching out to the child. Mamma's relationship with her husband will also be affected, as valuing material things and appearances over emotionally connecting to others harms the closeness of any relationship, and a need for a certain perceived standard of life seems to take preference here.

Dadda we hear is 'very affectionate' and 'lovely to us'. We hear how he loved his working environment, telling us he is a social person. Mamma and Dadda are presented as complete opposites. One of the theories of attraction is the concept of the opposite poles. All couples are recognised as having an opposite, and with my couples work it is always apparent. Opposite poles that draw together, like opposite poles of a magnet, attracting and pulling towards each other, then sticking together. But what draws us together can push us apart, as it can be difficult and frustrating living with opposite qualities to our own. This can be overcome if both partners can learn to understand and accept each other.

Mamma

We hear Ellen talking of the City gents when she visits the pub, saying 'it's quite posh' and Mamma believing it was the 'best thing' to be in Sudbury. When I read the little information we have on Mamma I cannot help but think the move from London to Sudbury was maybe more about it being right for Mamma than being right for the children. We are told Mamma is withdrawn, and finds it difficult to talk to people. 'No wonder she didn't like the rawness of London,' says Ellen.

'Show me a true Londoner and I'll show you a friend,' someone once said to me; and went on to recite some of their qualities: warm, genuine, open and no-nonsense, sharing their business like they've known you forever. For someone like Mamma this could have become a nightmare with her withdrawn and pretentious ways. Her home was a pub that she shared to an extent with a cleaner and a cook, and other bar staff would have been around. To actually work behind the bar with her husband would have been impossible for someone who finds it difficult to talk to people, especially when there are certain people not talked to at all. Later, in Sudbury, we hear the girls are not being allowed to play in the street, an activity that's the norm for the other children of the neighbourhood. ('They're rough' and 'It's not nice'.) This means they are deprived of the friendships that are the benefit of this, the opportunity to literally become 'streetwise' with their peers and discover their natural abilities; to learn independence.

This behaviour from Mamma, plus the insistence with the census man to present herself as having 'private means', tells us that Mamma was possibly a 'snob' in layman's terms, but in psychological terms this can be based on fear. Fear of what people might think if she presents herself in certain ways; fear she might be less of a person if she does not have certain behaviour or live in certain ways; fear of her children growing up in a way she finds negative; fear of not being the type of person she feels she should be. She cannot however let anyone see any of this, so she will cover it with bravado, presenting herself as better than others, and these certain standards of hers will say that she is. This behaviour is also a great stress producer, as energy is constantly used to preserve the status quo at the expense of genuineness. Being genuine is the easy way, as it's the truth about ourselves that flows with no effort.

If a person is secure, and can look honestly at themselves and their behaviour, and learn and grow as a person, they have no need to care about what other people think. Knowing and feeling that the self is 'OK' they can go through life recognising the falseness in others, and anyone who judges others is deemed as having a

17

problem, and will not generally be entertained in the secure person's life. Are you comfortable in your own skin? Mamma doesn't sound happy in hers and felt that if she could surround herself with 'niceness' and material things then she would be OK. We don't need expensive objects to feel secure and show people we are of value. To value ourselves is to have security.

It is worth mentioning here one of the results of an over-protective childhood. Clients with anxiety have very often traced this back to an over-protective parent or carer, giving the child the message that the world is not a safe place. After all, why else would I not be allowed to go out in it? The child can pick up the parents' anxieties too. The message that the world is not a safe place and a sensing of a parent's anxiety can be a very insecure situation for a child, who needs to know that his world is secure and stable within the family.

As the child senses a parent's anxiety, they do not have any further information and can imagine and fear all sorts of scary things that may be out there. As a result of this the foundations are not laid for security, so when the child has grown up, the childhood fears can resurface again. However, Ellen's childhood is not generally over-protective. The children are walking several miles a day by themselves and are put on the train to London, but limiting their contact with their peers can have an effect on social development which can cause the children to feel different from their peers, and can encourage a naivety and a lack of confidence.

Ellen and George

What has drawn Ellen and George together?

'It's a weird thing, this unconscious attraction stuff,' said a client one day after exploring the similarities between his partner and various members of his dysfunctional family.

The theory of attraction that I use in relationship work is an interesting one, and I have never failed to find evidence of it when working with clients. The opposite poles theory always seems to be present but the predominant pattern is that of unconsciously attracting someone who has experienced a similar background to ourselves. By 'background' we mean our family or carers' person-alities, and our experiences. Because these can be so familiar, we very often do not recognise any early signs. Something familiar to us that is negative is often not recognised until it becomes quite strong, and if we are needy, desperate or just plain romantic we can ignore the warning signs anyway, wanting to continue with the nice parts of a new relationship. Later we can start to feel and recognise certain behaviours, and very often if these behaviours are negative it can be too late, as we have now bonded with the other person and it becomes painful to leave. This can be why people stay in unhappy relationships often for a lot longer than they need to. If we are desperate and needy as well, we seem to attract and are attracted to the worst similarities we have in common from our backgrounds. 'But he was lovely when I met him!' 'She never did that in the beginning!' are common cries. 'That's because you had only experienced one part,' I have gently pointed out on so many occasions. We have many different parts of ourselves and over time, with various experiences and environments, the other parts become apparent. It can take a long time to get to know someone properly.

Can George and Ellen give each other what they need? Being needy and vulnerable often means it can be ultimately impossible to give, as we need so badly to receive, and both will need the same thing. Both George and Ellen are vulnerable and needy. Both have no secure close family at the time of their meeting, George having cut off from his, and Ellen, although in the same city as her father, has lost her original close family, and with the death of her mother and now her sister, she has recently moved to yet another environ-ment. George and Ellen both lost their mothers at the same age. When George cut off from his family, he was grieving the death of his mother and angry with his father. George was close to his mother – maybe closer than his siblings, as her death and the subsequent behaviour of his father obviously affected him very deeply.

Ellen has been forced to leave her family home where she was brought up and has moved many miles away to London. Even given the choice of whether to stay in Sudbury with the family she loved, or move to London, it would have been a hard one, as Ellen loved her father dearly and had never been able to live near him before. Now Ellen has also lost her close sister Grace who she has been with ever since she can remember. She and Gracie had been through everything together. She wouldn't remember a time when Gracie wasn't there. What with losing Mamma, leaving the family, and all the moving around, the loss of Gracie would have hit hard. What we take for granted today with healthcare, vaccinations, hospitals and medicine was not available during Ellen's childhood. Both her mother and sister died at home from TB.

George and Ellen come from the same country town, sharing a history of similarity. It is easy for them both, after their losses, to feel they are alone in the world physically and emotionally. On top of all this, George is fighting in the Great War and is to experience its horrors and hardships.

'He made me laugh.' 'It was just what I needed.' George comes into Ellen's life at the right time, to help her in her grief for Gracie, but there needs to be a balance. Can George share his own grief with Ellen? Asking for help gives opportunity for the fulfillment of giving on both sides. Intimate relating means sharing parts of ourselves.

Ellen and George unconsciously recognise all their similar experiences, are attracted, and cling together. Marrying George when the war is still on and 'no one knew whether they would live or die', Ellen says she soon realised she had made a mistake. A hasty marriage means there is no courtship; no time for the couple to get to know each other.

It can be far easier to find happiness in the present day with the normality of living together before marriage, but in the days of Ellen and George, marriage was the norm and co-habiting was termed 'living in sin', not generally considered to be the right thing to do. There was no contraception widely available; no birth control clinics. Sex before marriage was a risky business and many went to the altar already pregnant, often marrying because it was the 'right thing'. Suddenly married and living together, George and Ellen will get to know each other, what it's like to have sex, what their expectations are and their outlook on life. Divorce in Ellen and George's time was virtually unheard of and was certainly not for the ordinary working man. It carried a stigma, but it was also financially out of reach, being very expensive as it involved the courts. Ellen's parents organised their own 'divorce'. Mamma was able to take her daughters and live with her sister, and Dadda supported them financially. There would have been no welfare benefits in those days, no help for single parents, and not everyone would have had somewhere to go. Women were generally dependent on men as there was no Equality Act, and many jobs were for men only. So in Ellen and George's day, it was not usually possible to leave an unhappy marriage. 'I made my life in my children,' says Ellen.

The more desperate and alone we feel in the world, the more we can desperately cling on to someone who suddenly appears in our life. We can understand this by imagining we are all alone in a culture of aliens; we can't speak the language; they don't live their lives as we do. The feelings of loneliness and isolation can be all-consuming. Suddenly we see another human. We are so excited and relieved. Our panic and fear is abated as we rush to this person, regardless of who they are. We feel we have found the connection for ourselves that we need so badly. This person also needs us as badly as we need them, and we cling to each other regardless of who we are as two separate people. As time goes by, we realise that there are differences and blocks between us. We become fearful again, and there can also be anger as we feel we have been let down, but we fear to leave this person because of the alternative.

Making a happy life, getting to know oneself and form-ing connections with other people before we enter a committed relationship with a sexual partner, means that the alternative is not feared or shunned.

George's Question

If George were coming to see me today he would typically have asked why his father behaved as he did.

Before we look at his father's behaviour, marrying 'a young girl not much older than George himself' very shortly, almost immediately, after his wife died, we have to acknowledge the times and how different it is today. It wasn't until 1929 that the age for marriage by parental consent was raised to sixteen; the age at this time in the story was twelve for a girl and fourteen for a boy.

George's father's behaviour could be a grief reaction. Some people deal with loss by immediate replacement and the choice is not always considered a sane one. We are more likely to make an unwise decision when we are needy, desperate and trying to suppress pain, instead of going through the grieving process.

Another reason for this behaviour could be a reflection of his father's immature personality. 'Age has nothing to do with maturity,' my grandmother would say, and it's true. An immaturity in personality can produce childish behaviour in certain environments throughout life. Many female clients with eventual relationship problems who have married someone with a big age gap, often one of around thirty years, find that the mature father figure they were seeking at the time has been a disappointment. A person can present as mature in their everyday life, but when it comes to close relating, if that part of the personality is immature, their mature partner will find unfulfilled relating.

A third possible reason for George's father's behaviour could be a desperate attempt to find a surrogate mother to bring up his children. We have to remember these were Edwardian times, with no labour-saving devices in the home, no fridges or freezers to make life easier, no benefits for single parents, and long working hours.

George's father would have needed to keep working to feed and clothe his growing family. Fears of poverty and the workhouse could cause many behaviours we may struggle to understand today. If George were able to interact with me now, he would be able to reach his own conclusion as to which reason was the right one, and this would help him to understand his father, and maybe to face the reality of what sort of person his father really is.

A mention of immature behaviour to a client, explaining that it often comes with a selfish personality trait, can bring an outpouring of past similar behaviours. It is as if permission has been given for this to be acknowledged and voiced, so finally the 'real' parent can be faced. Similarly, understanding grief reactions or realising survival techniques can bring empathy as we start to see the event through the eyes of an adult, and are eventually able to understand the behaviour. Any one of these would have helped George to see the situation in a different way, and start to dissipate the anger. George would have been encouraged to talk about his father and mother, and voice the anger and sadness he felt. He would have been given a 'discharge book': a blank exercise book to write down any thoughts and feelings that may come to him in-between therapy sessions, to help discharge them. If there was anyone George could share his feelings with, he would have been encouraged to do so, and if there were certain things that felt too uncomfortable for him to talk about or voice, then I would have encouraged him to write them in his book, using any words he wishes. If writing is a problem then pictures and diagrams can be used. There is no requirement for correct spelling, or judgment of words used or pictures drawn.

Keeping the book in a private place just for him, he would have had the choice whether to bring it to sessions to work with and maybe understand more about what happened, or just keep the book in private for his own use.

Apart from George being already full of this anger and grief, other experiences in the Great War will add to these feelings; 'The war that scarred a generation.' Many men returned never to speak of their experiences over a whole lifetime. Unless he can find an outlet for all these feelings by sharing them and expressing them in a healthy way, George is likely to display stress reactions in the future. More stress building up over time with other negative life events, and George could also be a likely candidate for depression. Ellen has been able to grieve and release emotion: 'We talked about Gracie a lot, and I cried and cried.'

Carrying strong feelings takes energy, and given too much to carry, we can start to shut down, causing withdrawn behaviour and in the extreme, a severe depression with an inability to function within normal life.

If George can talk to Ellen about his mother, and voice his feelings about his father, this will help him to discharge feelings and work through his grief and anger. If he can keep a diary too then even better, as writing brings much release, and can sort out feelings. George may have been putting his own grief on hold in the attempt to be there for Ellen, trying to make her feel better; 'He made me laugh, it was just what I needed.'

How will George and Ellen's marriage be? How will they bring up their children? What sort of life are they destined to have together? Why was it a mistake for Ellen?

The next story, told through the eyes of their first child, Mary, explains more about what happened after they married.

The Mother's Story (Mary)

A Suffolk Childhood

My mother Ellen had given up work when she married as that was considered the 'done thing' in those days, if you could afford it. We lived in Sudbury, my father's family being well known, as his father – my grandfather – owned a building business and had built several properties in the town. I never knew this grandfather. My grandmother had died at forty-four, and my grandfather had married again very suddenly, almost immediately, to a very young woman, not much older than my father who was then fifteen. My father had been so angry and full of grief that he had severed all connections with the family and run away to join the army, lying about his age. The Great War had begun. Because of this I also never met his brother, my Uncle Ben, although he lived not far from us. His sister Rose, who he had been close to as a child, eventually reunited with us by contacting my mother. After the meetings that followed, we would go to visit her. Aunty Rose was such a nice, jolly person. I always felt sad there were upsets in the family, and just wished they would all speak to each other. Sometimes we visited my father's aunt, also called Rose, who lived in a tiny cottage with chickens at the bottom of the garden. Next to the chickens was the outside toilet, so when we stayed the night, which my sister Lizzie and I sometimes did, sleeping at the bottom of Aunt Rose's bed on a feather mattress, we had to be sure we didn't want to 'go' after we'd gone to bed, or it meant walking down the garden in the dark and cold. At home we had 'potties' under the beds for this: china pots with handles.

25

There was no electricity at Aunt Rose's, just oil lamps. I remember lots of tassels on the furniture, all the chairs and the sofa were horsehair and very hard and uncomfortable. Aunt Rose had long black skirts, black boots and her hair in a bun with a hat that had a hatpin sticking out. Uncle Arch didn't go to work as he had some disability from the Great War, but would sit in front of a frame sewing the most beautiful tapestries, which were sold for the benefit of injured soldiers.

My mother was born at the Queen's Head Hotel in Putney, where her father was working as a barman and her mother was a servant. They both 'lived in' and already had her sister, Grace. Their father had been able to get a manager's job at the East India Arms in the City, which was a tall, narrow building, with rooms on four floors. There was an attic room at the top with a marvellous view over London. As children, we would sometimes visit Granddad on Sundays when the pub was closed. He was married to Rosa who we called Nana, but it wasn't our real nana. She had died a very long time ago, and Granddad had eventually married again. Rosa was lovely to us, just like we were her real grandchildren.

We thought she was very glamorous, with her jewellery and lipstick, and we said she looked like she never did any housework, and she probably didn't as there was a cleaner who lived in the pub who also cooked. It was such a shock to us when we heard that Nana had fallen down the iron spiral staircase, and died. She was ill at the time with bronchitis and after quite a time in bed had probably got a bit fed up and went to go down to the bar where my granddad was working, as usual. The cleaner saw her, remonstrating that she should be in bed, and then she stumbled and fell from top to bottom. She broke her neck, and was certified dead at the scene. They had been married for thirteen years.

When my parents married, my father started his own building business, which became very successful. We had a gold plate on the door that said: 'George Charles Joshua Gooday, Builder, Decorator and Undertaker'. I understood all the names were important so as not to be confused with his father, also called George, who still conducted the original family business. There was never any trouble; we just never had anything to do with them. The undertaker part was an extra, apparently, as there was a demand for one in the town. We lived in a very large house called York House. It had lots of outbuildings for workshops, and the building materials were transported in handcarts. There was a storeroom with loads of wallpaper, and customers would come in and choose what they wanted. One of the outbuildings was used as a morgue for the undertaking part of the business. The bodies would be placed in this little building prior to burial. When my brother Will was very young, he worried and worried my father to show him a dead body. My father eventually relented and my mother was furious. Will had a natural curiosity and it didn't seem to do him any harm. I never wanted to see one. A familiar sight for me was my father cycling up to the cemetery at the top of the hill with a tiny baby coffin on the handlebars for the burial. We never thought anything of it; it was part of life. All the coffins were made in the workshops next to the house, and in one workshop was a wardrobe with top hats and formal outfits that the workmen would wear to the funerals to act as bearers, my father walking in front of the coffin in a large top hat and black coat.

I adored York House. I knew we were lucky to be living in it, as none of my friends' houses were so big. Entering the front door you went straight into a large sitting room, which then led into a large dining room, then into a large kitchen. My father had arranged it like this by knocking down an inside wall to get rid of the long, draughty hall that ran from front to back. In winter, the warmest room was always the kitchen as it had a large solid-fuel range that was the cooker and also heated the hot water. Later, we had a gas cooker as well. There was a large stone sink with both hot and cold taps, and also the original pump which still pumped water from a well. In the back lobby where we kept all the coats and shoes there was a wall telephone that I would sometimes stand on a chair to answer, when my mother was busy and my father was out working. There was also a cellar, a very exciting place, as it was very dark, and one room had a hole in the top. We would stand at the cellar steps watching from afar as the coal would be tipped down from the street above, making an almighty roar and clouds of black dust. From the kitchen we could see across the yard my father's office, and when I got older, about ten, I would help stick the stamps on the men's work cards and sometimes was allowed to put the wages in the envelopes. They would all line up for their pay on a Saturday morning, each name called in turn.

My sister Lizzie was born when I was fourteen months old, so I don't ever remember a time when she wasn't there. When I was three, my brother Will was born at home like nearly all babies were, and one of my mother's friends had moved in to help. I took an instant dislike to her, and missed my mother not being around as she usually was. I was not allowed to 'trouble' my mother, and one day I crept upstairs and opened her bedroom door. There was a cot by the bed which I ignored as it was my mother I wanted. She gave me a chocolate from a box on the bedside table and then in came the friend! She told me off for being there and sent me away. I was so miserable and furious I ran downstairs to the bottom of the garden where I sat on the swing, my father digging nearby, and holding the chocolate in my hand whilst grasping the swing rope, I squashed it to pieces.

The garden was a marvellous place: a big open space with paving at the top, opening out into a huge lawn where we would play ball, skip with our skipping ropes, play hopscotch or just tear around. My father did a lot of gardening, growing vegetables and fruit bushes. We had redcurrants, blackcurrants, gooseberries and strawberries. Fruit trees ran along the high walls at the side. There was a greenhouse at the bottom where we had a grapevine. I remember eating these grapes for breakfast, all freshly picked and warm. We would spend hours picking the fruit and also peas and beans. My mother would bottle a lot of the fruit for the winter. Hidden away in the corner at the bottom was a triangular summer house. I was able to climb on to the roof, and would sit looking over the rectory garden next door. It wasn't very exciting though, as nothing ever happened. They had two boys who always seemed to be away at boarding school. We never played outside in the street and looking back, I suppose we didn't need to, but there were a couple of streets where we were not allowed to go, or talk to the children there. These streets had poor people living in them and we were told they were 'rough'.

My brother Harry was also born at home, when I was eight. I was awakened very early by my mother telling me to dress quickly and go and tell my father to come at once. He was always up early and was in the workshop. Later I remember the baby being brought to us in the kitchen. Again we had someone to come in and look after us, who also brought her sixteen-year-old daughter to help and once again, I greatly resented this. I would call them names, out of earshot I hope now, and I remember being very difficult and uncooperative. I never resented my brothers and sisters though, and we were always happy together as a family.

I had a great love of reading and would shut myself away for long periods, my mother worriedly coming to check on me now and again, as I often felt I wanted to be by myself. There were lots of books in the house; a lot were grown-up books, which I got through, never really understanding the full meaning. I also went to the library and we had annuals and children's books for presents.

There were constant visitors. Aunty Kate, my mother's cousin – they were brought up together – would often come to stay with her husband Uncle Charlie. My mother said Aunty Kate had married a 'cockney'. We weren't sure what this was but thought it must be someone who came from London as that was who Uncle Charlie was; he was bright, chirpy and funny. They had no children but were lovely when playing with us. We would all pile into their bed in the mornings and Aunty Kate would sing to us in her wonderful voice and Uncle Charlie would recite funny rhymes to us. Grand-dad would sometimes come on his days off from the East India Arms. Two of my mother's friends visited from Shoreditch in London. They ran a milk delivery business with their parents, and the cows were kept in a field in Shoreditch with the horse, which pulled the cart with the churns on. People would come out of their houses with their jugs to be filled. These two friends stayed the night and one of them woke early and came downstairs for a drink of water. Opening the cellar door thinking it was the kitchen, she fell to the bottom of the stairs, luckily not badly hurt, but they never came again. Aunty Nellie and Uncle John would come with their two boys from Bury St Edmunds, where they ran a men's outfitters' shop. Then another time Uncle John would come in his car and take us to their large, rambling flat where they lived above the shop. It was very unusual to have a car. Uncle John was the only person we knew who had one.

My mother was a wonderful person, bringing up four of us at a time when mostly there was no electricity. I remember she had the first type of washing machine, a big tub where you had to push the handle from side to side. A bit later what seemed like a very old lady would come on a bike from one of the villages and clean in the house, two days a week. My mother was an excellent cook and she must have spent hours at it, as we all – including my father – came home to lunch, which was the main dinner of the day. There were often visitors joining us, too. My father had very strict rules at the meal table. No talking was allowed and he must have had a strong influence on all of us as we kept silent. Sometimes we were wary of him, as he could suddenly be irritable and short with us; other times he would be jokey and funny, but you never knew how it was going to be. When we went out as a family, we had to behave in a certain way, and we all did, so we sensed that it was best to obey.

Besides bottling all the fruits from the garden, my mother made all the jams. Every Sunday after cooking the lunch she made a large pink and white coconut ice, which we soon devoured, and also a large cake. We always had a large joint of meat on Sundays and my father would carve at the head of the table. The first course was a large slice of York-shire pudding with delicious gravy and I thought this was the best part, not thinking much of the meat and veg to follow.

My mother, being a professional needlewoman before she married, also found time to make all our clothes. She had a gift to be able to give time to each of us children, to listen to our problems, and I suppose because I was the eldest she confided in me too and we were very close. I liked to help and please her, and remember ironing with the various irons heating on the range in the kitchen, lifting off a hot one and then replacing it to heat up again, then taking off another.

My father, apart from working at his building business and the garden, was a lover of sport, and found time to be in the cricket team in the summer and played football in the winter. I remember once going to a regatta on the river where he was rowing.

When I was seven we suddenly owned a car. One of my father's friends had persuaded him he needed a car and sold him his second-hand one. There was no driving test in those days; he was just given instructions by this friend. I suppose it was OK because there were hardly any cars on the road. It meant we sometimes had a Sunday outing to the seaside at Clacton, which was very exciting as none of our friends had this.

Sudbury was a market town with a large market and a cattle market every Thursday, when the cattle would walk along the roads to the market from the outlying villages. Sometimes we would hear of a bull running loose in the town.

It was lovely in the market at Christmas. The stalls were open long after dark and large naked flares were hung on them for lighting. My father always took us there on the Saturday before Christmas, the lights glowing, and we would chose decorations for the house, and little chocolates for the tree.

One Christmas was different as Lizzie caught diphtheria, a very serious illness in those days, as there were no inoculations. The hospital was miles out into the country, in isolation because of the risk of infection, so my father and mother couldn't visit very often and when they did, they were only allowed to look through a window at Lizzie. My father was glad he had the car then.

That Christmas, we all piled into the car and set off very early in the morning to visit Lizzie in hospital. We children had to wait in the car, as we weren't allowed to look through the window at Lizzie. I did wonder how she felt, away from the family, especially at Christmas. From there we drove on to Kingston in London to visit my mother's uncle and aunt, who she had once lived with many years ago. I remember the car getting stuck on tramlines as we came into London, and an angry tram driver shouting at my father, but we must have extricated ourselves as we stayed a couple of nights with Aunty and Uncle. When Lizzie eventually came home from hospital, she was full of such good tales about who she had met and what went on, that I wished I could go there too. Unfortunately my wish came true as not long after, I also contracted diphtheria, and spent my eighth birthday there. I remember being delirious, seeing strange things on the walls and being in an ambulance. Once I was aware of my surroundings I didn't find it attractive at all and couldn't get home quick enough.

It wasn't long after that my father was driving down Acton Lane, which was quite narrow, and met a coach on a corner. He ended up being thrust into the bank with a broken arm and many cuts to his face. He never drove again.

One day, I remember we were having dinner in the dining room when suddenly Lizzie shrieked, and we all followed her eyes to the ceiling to see a wire poking through and wiggling at us. There was great excitement as we were told the house was being wired for electric light. A year or so later our first wireless set was put on the table and we heard music and people talking. It had very large batteries, which had to be taken to a shop to be recharged. This opened a whole new world for me and was the start of a lifelong love of music, as I never had heard such marvellous singing and wonderful orchestras as came through the wireless.

Harry was sent to school a lot later than me, Lizzie and Will, who all started at three, but Harry was nearly six. 'I like having him at home with me, I don't want him to go yet!' my mother would say to me.

At ten, I entered for a scholarship to get to the high school. I was determined to go because I had decided I definitely could not stay at the council school. I wanted to do clever things, I loved maths; maybe I would go to university. You could pay to go to the high school, but my mother and father wouldn't pay for girls, only the boys. This was quite normal in those days as it was considered a waste of time paying for girls, as they would only get married. I would have liked to work in a bank but no women were allowed to work in banks, which seems unbelievable now. I passed the scholarship and once I was at the high school, I realised there were others brainier than me and had to work hard in some subjects to keep up. Lizzie took the scholarship and failed, which I never understood as she was so much better at English than me. She really needed to pass as she wanted to be a nurse and the school certificate was essential to be taken on for the training. However, she couldn't be paid for, as that was only for the boys. It was lucky for her that when war was declared, hospitals changed their ideas, and she eventually became a trained nurse.

The high school I attended was a lovely old double-fronted house with many beams. We had a small tarmac playground on one side and a grass tennis court on the other. We had to walk through the town to the boys' grammar school to use their playing fields for hockey, returning muddy and tired. Eventually a new, much bigger school was built, and we had our own playing fields and showers for the hockey days.

It was at the end of my first year at high school when the blow fell. My father lost all his money. He had taken a contract for building houses down in Kent, paying for himself and his workmen to lodge. When the time came for payment he didn't receive any. The customer had gone bankrupt. We were going to have to move from York House and all the workmen lost their jobs. The house and most of the building stock would have to pay the bills. Later I was told that if my father had confided in his friend Uncle John, then he could have helped us remain where we were, but my father would never confide in others or talk over his problems. Uncle John however did find us a house to rent at a much-reduced rate in Friar Street, which had a workshop, an office and an open yard. What Uncle John hadn't known, though, was that this was the same house my father had been brought up in, the one he ran away from when his mother died. When we moved into this house it was the blackest day of my life.

During the following years, my father seemed a lot quieter and even more remote from us; looking back I think he may have been depressed. My mother was devastated by the change. A tiny kitchen with no range for hot water, only cold, my father lighting the gas copper to heat the water on wash days, and once a week to fill the bath for us all, which was in a tiny room next to the kitchen. Everywhere was so much smaller for her growing family and she had no help in the house like she had before. There was far less money, but meals appeared as miraculously as before. We had less clothes but she spent hours on the sewing machine so we could have party frocks and anything else special that was required. Sometimes she would be ill and need to rest; I would then try out my cooking skills on the rest of the family as she had taught me, often taking the big yellow mixing bowl up to the bedroom where she lay, to ask her about a consistency of this or that. Eventually she was diagnosed as anaemic and then many years later, at the age of eighty-six, chronic leukaemia appeared on the death certificate. I remember looking up 'chronic' in the medical sense, and found it meant slow growing. I'm sure she never knew she had it. There was not the treatment for things in those days or the facility for diagnosis. However she lived a very long life, considering all the hardships.

The worst thing of all about this house for us children was that there was no garden. That beautiful space we had to play and dream was gone and now there was only a builders' yard with a workshop and an office. My mother however was offered a tiny piece of land down a lane to grow vegetables and she planted lots of flowers and made a lovely little garden where she would escape when the house became too depressing. The years at York House had made a great impression on me, and are more real to me than the following years of my childhood. I had been heartbroken when we were told we would have to leave it; the memories of it never left me, and for many years I would have recurring dreams at night of living there again and then would awake to reality and great sorrow.

Sudbury however was a good town to live in. I enjoyed being near all the shops, and the cinema. There was the Victoria Hall where amateur dramatics would be staged and the town hall had occasional concerts of bands and small orchestras. I would sometimes be allowed to go to these.

The swimming pool was our delight. Not as you would probably imagine it, as it was part of the River Stour, which ran through the Sudbury meadows! The river was slightly tidal so it was deeper at some times than others. A concrete base had been constructed on one side of the river and wooden changing huts were built. There was also a concrete base put in the river, but only as far as the changing huts went. Further than this and you would encounter weeds and the occasional fish, which could be a large pike! On the other side of the river they built concrete steps going down into the water, and the two sides were linked by a bridge which we used as a diving board! As cattle drank from the river and also frequently walked in it too, it was not healthy for children and I know now there were cases of polio. Generations of children had learned to swim in that river. We would spend hours there in the summer. Eventually, the health authorities closed it down and a new proper swimming pool was built in the town. It was very modern for those days but still outside and unheated!

With no garden, the meadows became our playground. The railway circled the meadows and we would wait for the steam trains. We would walk miles exploring and found many places for good blackberrying in the late summer, coming home laden. We would paddle in some parts of the river and take jam jars and fishing nets to catch the tiddlers.

Then eventually after about three years, good news, we were moving again. A friend of mine lived in a larger house a little further outside of the town centre, which was becoming available for rent. My father had managed to build up his business again to an extent where we could now afford it. My mother was overjoyed. It had a very large garden, was semi-detached and in a quiet road overlooking the meadows. But we still had the copper and worse, a tin bath hanging on a wall outside which had to be brought in and filled once a week from the copper. Also an outside toilet for the first time, but my mother was so overjoyed at the space and where it was, that she coped with these problems with ease. There was no workshop for my father but he managed to hire one at the end of the road. My father built around the outside toilet so it was now inside and there was a 'wash house' and a bath. The year after that, war was declared and he joined the army.

During these years, I worked towards my school certificate. However I got more and more disheartened as I realised my dream of university would never happen. My money was needed at home, and anyway they would never pay for me to go to university, only the boys, and there were no grants. I passed but then left school at fifteen. I remember shedding tears when I had to leave.

If I couldn't go to university, I wanted some other adventure and decided I would leave home for work. I managed to get a post as an 'under-nursemaid' for a family in Hertfordshire. The father was a 'Hon' and we called them upper class. I was however very miserable, as most of the time I was required to do cleaning which I hated, and saw very little of the children. I left after only three weeks and went to stay with Aunty Kate in London. She knew someone who ran a boarding school in Kent and managed to get me a job as a teacher to the younger ones, with an age range of three to seven. I had no training for any of it, and today would be regarded as a child myself. The fact that I had the school certificate was supposed to be enough. It was very difficult keeping the three-year-old occupied, and one seven-year-old was slightly retarded and couldn't concentrate properly. I shared a bedroom with the two youngest boys, although I did have a curtain around my area of the room. Apart from getting them all up in the morning, I also had to take them for a walk before lunch, supervise tea, and then see them to bed. My meal was then brought to me on a tray. In between all of this I taught them, or tried to teach them, the basics of reading, writing and numbers. I felt very sorry for them and wondered where their parents were, and why they had to leave them in what to me seemed a very uninteresting place. On Mondays I had to wash their clothes, but I didn't mind as it was a relief to have a change from the classroom. On Sundays we took them all to church. I had one day off a month, and half a day off a week. I suddenly realised that I was becoming very homesick, and got my mother to write to the Head (who was Aunty Kate's friend and had done me a favour) saying I was needed urgently at home. I arrived back in time for Christmas and decided I never wanted to go away again!

I managed to get a job in the silk factory in Sudbury, this having been a big industry in the area for many years. I designed men's ties and scarves, and quite enjoyed it. Meanwhile, however, war had been declared and my father was away in the army. I suddenly decided I wanted to join up too; I was feeling ready for more adventure.

The War Years

My mother, on hearing of my plan to join up, managed to persuade me to stay at home until Christmas was over, as my father George was already away, so it was the day after Boxing Day, 27th December 1942, that I left Sudbury on the early morning train to London. Waterloo Station, where I was heading, was closed as it had been hit during an air raid in the night. Luckily I knew London quite well because of Granddad at the East India Arms and Aunty Kate, so I managed to find a bus to Clapham Junction where the trains were running and would take me to Bournemouth, where I had been instructed to report. I was joining the ATS: the Auxiliary Territorial Service, which was the army for women. Lizzie wanted to join the air force but I was following my father into the army.

It was quite a relief to meet three other girls on the train who were going to the same place as I was, which turned out to be a big hotel on the Bournemouth sea front. It wasn't a hotel now though, as the army had requisitioned it for training. We were shown to the bedrooms, which had as many beds crammed into each one as possible. There was no other furniture, and the kit bags we were issued with had to be used to keep all our belongings in. We hadn't been in bed more than a couple of hours when suddenly there was an air raid warning and we all dragged our mattresses downstairs and slept in the basement. There wasn't much sleep as we could hear planes continuously; we were told they were heading for Southampton, which was the target that night.

Our days in Bournemouth were filled with lectures and route marches. We were free at weekends and explored Bournemouth, having tea out, but had to be back always by 7 p.m. Eventually I was interviewed by an officer to see what sort of work I was suited for. She suggested teleprinting and signals work, which I knew very little about but thought that it might be all right.

The signals school was a few miles along the coast and one other girl, Vicky, came with me. Vicky and I were complete opposites. She never stopped talking and was the life of any group or party. I was much quieter, a bit more serious and wasn't comfortable being loud in groups. Against all odds we became great friends, which lasted a whole lifetime.

We learned touch-typing on typewriters to start with and then transferred to the teleprinters, receiving and sending messages. We learned messaging in Morse code and also telephone work. I enjoyed it, found it interesting and felt I was really doing something to be part of the war, helping to win.

Vicky and I passed the end exams, had a pay increase, and were transferred to Wilton House, Salisbury – the headquarters of Southern Command.

Wilton House was a stately home, where huts had been built in the grounds to accommodate the signals work. We did day shifts, catching the bus from our hotel lodgings, returning in the back of an army lorry. The men did the night shifts.

There was a swimming pool that we used, and we enjoyed exploring Salisbury and the surrounding meadows on our day off. After only two weeks however, Vicky was transferred to a very large army camp at Ashchurch. I felt very glad it wasn't me.

The friends I made during the next few months were also friendships that lasted a lifetime. I met Kay, a telephonist, when Vicky had gone. She was getting married and I managed to get time off and went to her wedding in Kingston, London. Suddenly I was posted to Oxford and there met Coullie, a Scottish girl. I went to stay with her in Scotland when the war had ended and we wrote to each other until she died in 1970. Oxford was a beautiful place to be and where I made another lasting friend, Joan. We managed to acquire second-hand bikes and spent our time off riding around the historical town, along the river, and out into the countryside. Joan eventually married, had a baby and lived in Alton, Hampshire. I visited her once and am still writing to her, forty years later.

Finally I learned I was to become an instructor, and was being sent to a mixed signals school in Putney, London. First however, I was told I could go home for Christmas. My mother was delighted and so were the boys. My sister Lizzie had just joined up and was away in the RAF nursing, and she and my father were unable to get home for Christmas.

After a cosy, warm, family Christmas it was back to reality at Putney. It was an old school with no electricity, only gaslight. There were bare floorboards and no heating, and as it was January and snowing, I felt this acutely. There were no bathrooms and I had to heat water in a kettle on a gas ring, and wash in a bowl on the landing. One night I was awakened by a noise, switched on my torch and a mouse jumped right across my face. The place was overrun with mice! When the blackouts were in force it was quite spooky, surrounded by huge bushes.

As it was quite near Kingston I would catch the bus to visit Kay's mother and stepfather every Sunday, for a lovely Sunday lunch and also tea, and then after that we would all go down to the 'local' and have drinks until it was time for me to catch the last bus back to Putney, braving the spooky corridors and stairs to get to my room. Then a really nice thing happened. Vicky joined me. She had been posted from Ashchurch and was determined we would try to get different accommodation. Somehow she managed to arrange for us to be transferred to a block of flats on the edge of Putney Heath. It was spacious and we were able to share a room. All our meals were provided at the Territorial Army complex opposite. I still had my second-hand bike, which I had brought from Oxford, so was able to cycle to the school every day to work. As it was a mixed battalion, I taught mainly men. My job was lecturing on 'Electricity and Magnetism', and teaching touch-typing to prepare them for teleprinter work. Looking back, I often wondered what the men thought, being taught by such a young ATS. I'm sure some of them must have known more than I did!

Being in London was lovely. I could visit Aunty Kate and also Granddad at the East India Arms. He had stayed there all through the Blitz in 1940, the ferocious attack on London by the German air force when around 20,000 people were killed. I visited him regularly, and then suddenly he became ill. It was three years after Rosa tragically fell down the iron stairs. My mother took him to Sudbury to look after him, turning the front sitting room into a bedroom. My father was given leave to help, and I was also given compassionate leave for a while. I had only been home a week when suddenly he died, very peacefully one morning. He had bronchitis and also emphysema which I thought only miners got, but my mother said it was being in the closed smoke-filled atmosphere of the bar for virtually his whole life, working in a fug she called it, and it seemed everyone smoked a pipe or cigarettes. I don't know whether anyone had connected lung illness with this then, but she had. I stayed for the funeral, and then had to return to Putney. When I returned there was a new instructor in the mess: Frank. Little did I know this was going to be the most important relationship of my life.

Frank and I soon realised we had a lot in common, with a love of music and concerts. He also had a bike and loved to cycle around to look at historical places, like I did. In another way we were complete opposites, a bit like me and Vicky. He was very talkative, and loved to be in a party crowd. He'd only been there a few days and was already putting on a social. I didn't go to this as I had decided to travel home for my birthday.

Frank had just come back from the Far East on compassionate leave. He had received the order without any information of why, or what had happened at home. He hadn't wanted to leave Ceylon where he had been stationed, as he was with all his mates, and enjoying the signals work out there. It had taken him a long time to get home, about three months. It had been a long haul by sea around the Cape as the Suez Canal was closed. When he eventually arrived home he was shocked to find his father dead at forty-seven, and his mother in a mental asylum. His father had been diagnosed with brain cancer and had died after a very short time. Just before this had happened his mother had received a war telegram saying that her only son Frank was reported missing presumed dead. The strain and shock of it all had caused her a mental breakdown. When his mother saw him it was the start of a very slow recovery. Frank was to work at the signals school for six months, and then when his mother was well enough to return home, he was allowed to work at his old job at Leicester Square post office, as a counter clerk. It meant he could travel from home to work every day in the week, and be with her all the time at weekends. I went with Frank to see him off at London Bridge station, to catch the train to Surrey when his mother was back in the family home. He suggested we should write to each other and said he would also occasionally be able to meet me after work.

I was then sent for a while to do some top-secret war work in a disused tunnel under Goodge Street station. It was the start of SHAEF – Supreme Headquarters Allied Expeditionary Force – a second front was being discussed. We were bound to secrecy. In this tunnel were kitchens and a dining room, as well as offices and lots of teleprinters and Morse code machines. This was especially good as it meant I was only a short distance away from Leicester Square where Frank was working. One evening we were having a meal in the Lyons Corner House at Charing Cross when he asked if I would go out with him seriously. I said yes! Afterwards, I went with him to London Bridge where he had to catch his train back home. While we were there we heard a peculiar noise in the sky and a funny looking thing like a small plane came over. A huge bang came soon after. This was the start of the fly bombs. It was one of the first of hundreds and they caused much destruction.

Whilst I was working at Goodge Street I was sharing a large house with five others opposite Regents Park Zoo. One evening we had just gone to bed when we heard this terrible noise coming over. I knew it was getting near the end and would fall. I shouted to everyone to get under the beds. Then the huge bang and all our windows were blown in, our beds completely covered with splintered glass from the large windows. We would certainly have been badly cut or worse. The bomb had fallen in the zoo opposite and several animals had been killed. These flying bombs carried on for months, and you just had to hope one didn't come down near you. Later they were overtaken by large rockets that just fell silently out of the sky with no warning, demolishing large areas. We were surrounded by them day and night, but just carried on as usual hoping we would survive.

Suddenly I was informed I was being moved again, to Bushey Park near Kingston. It was the new SHAEF headquarters and Eisenhower's base for the planning of D-Day. We lived and worked in huts in the grounds of Bushey Park. Secret letters which had been decoded were given to me to edit, to make in proper order as a letter, then they were passed on to the typists. I still met Frank when I could, in London after his shift at the post office. One Saturday afternoon we went to a concert in Wimbledon: Tchaikovsky's Piano Concerto No 1, which we both loved. We went for a walk afterwards on Wimbledon Common, and while we were sitting on a seat Frank proposed. I didn't have to think twice before I said yes. After that we always said the Tchaikovsky piano concerto was 'our tune'. We celebrated our engagement in Lyons Corner House with a few army friends we had managed to collect together.

I managed a day off to meet Frank's mother in Surrey, but then I was sent to Portsmouth, to work in a fort high on a hill overlooking the town. We had to sleep in tents, although the fort did have washing facilities and everything else we needed. It was the first time I had seen an electric typewriter. It was during this time that I thought Frank and I should get married when we could. We were constantly being moved apart, and we never knew whether we would live or die.

We decided on a date five months later, October 1st – a Sunday as most people were working on Saturdays. Kingston seemed the best place as my mother could travel from Sudbury and stay with Aunty Nellie at their old childhood home. Frank's mother could travel easily there from Surrey and Kay's family lived there too. Aunty Kate and Uncle Charlie weren't far away. My sister Lizzie was able to get leave to be my bridesmaid. The only thing I never thought would happen was that my father was unable to get leave. He and I were very disappointed that he wouldn't be able to give me away at my wedding. My brother Will stepped in, now also in the army and able to get leave to take his place. Harry was still at school, so would come with my mother. Kay's mother was marvellous and said she would have the reception at her house, and somehow with food short and rationed managed to provide enough sandwiches, and miraculously produced a wedding cake made with dried fruit which was almost unheard of. We decided to be posh and have one night at the Strand Palace Hotel, catching the train the next day to Ilfracombe for a short honeymoon. However, we didn't realise how much we loved the bustle and life of the city, as our hotel by the sea in wartime and in October was nearly empty apart from a few very elderly residents. The town seemed deserted. We invented a story to the very nice owner saying Frank had been recalled to the army and we had to leave immediately. We spent the remaining days at the Strand Palace, which had been so comfortable!

I had managed to get more leave for my wedding than Frank had, so when he had to report to Kirkburton in Yorkshire, I went with him. We were both able to be in lodgings near the camp and then they let him have another week before being posted to Europe. In Yorkshire we found that the shops were far more prolific with household articles than they were down south, so we bought ourselves plates, dishes, and bowls of all sizes, mainly Pyrex, and some real china dinner plates. Somehow we managed to carry it all back on the train plus our luggage, and get to Surrey, where we spent the remaining days of our leave with Frank's mother.

Meanwhile the war was slowly dragging on. Frank went to France and I went to live with his mother, travelling up on the train every day to Mayfair where I was now stationed, and where flying bombs were coming over constantly, and rockets causing intense damage. We just carried on with our work, travel and recreation as everyone else did. It didn't occur to me there might be a bomb 'with my name on'. As 1945 progressed the attacks lessened as our armies gained territories and were capturing the launching sites. Then in May the peace treaty was signed and there was great rejoicing. We were still at war with Japan though, so there wasn't complete demobilisation. My father was home quite quickly but Frank had to wait until 1946.

I was enjoying my work in London and decided to stay on, although I could have left immediately as married women were the first to go. After a while though it wasn't as exciting as in wartime, so I asked to be discharged. I then had to decide what to do until Frank came home.

As I was living with Frank's mother, I took a bus to Sutton post office and asked if they needed a teleprinter operator. Fortunately for me they did, and I did shift work sending and receiving messages, and taking down telegrams over the telephone. It was busy and I enjoyed it.

When Frank came home, there was no hope of getting a house of our own. So many houses had been destroyed during the war and no new ones had been built yet. Everyone seemed to be coming back from the services with nowhere to live. Frank's mother said we must stay with her, so she moved into the front room and we had the back room, sharing the kitchen and the bathroom. She gave up her large bedroom and had the smaller back room. We lived separately as far as general living arrangements went. This was the way of life for a lot of young couples then, especially those returning from the services. Any new furniture had to be bought with a set number of coupons, and we were able to buy a dining table, four chairs, a bed and a wardrobe. Household linen was on coupons too and we were only allowed three sheets, two on the bed and one in the wash. Food was even scarcer, and virtually everything was rationed so we became expert at making things go a long way.

Frank was working shifts at the post office, which included night duty, but when we did manage to be off work at the same time we would go for bike rides in the country. However we were all so pleased that the war was over, and that we were together forever, we never felt deprived of anything.

Years later when Frank had managed to catch up with his studying and had been promoted, we were suddenly offered a large house to rent in North London. It was the house of our dreams where we were to bring up our two children, Jillian and Andrew. We could only afford to sparsely furnish it at first, had mostly bare boards, and just managed to live from week to week, but we thought we were in heaven.

Under The Hood Part 2

Mary's Question

Mary never met her other grandfather, despite the fact he lived in the same town and was in the same kind of business as her father. She also never met her uncle, her father's brother. Eventually she did meet her aunt, her father's sister. 'I always felt sad there were upsets in the family, and just wished they could speak to each other.' Why couldn't they? Why didn't they?

It is Aunty Rose, George's sister, who finally manages to mend things for herself, by approaching Ellen. This shows us how difficult it was to approach George, and maybe she tried, maybe Ellen tried, maybe no one tried, knowing it would be fruitless. It also suggests that Aunty Rose is different from her brothers and her father. 'His sister Rose, who he had been close to as a child, eventually reunited with us by contacting my mother. After the meetings which followed, we would go to visit her.' We don't know how far her attempts went to mend this situation for all the family.

For George and his father to start speaking again under these circumstances, George's father would have had a lot of work to do. This is not only because of George's carried anger against him, but because it is a parent-child situation. Although George was no longer a child, the original problem is parent-child. George's strong feelings stem from that time and they will need to be addressed before any healing between them can be achieved. George's father would need to be able to acknowledge and understand George's anger, and be able to explain why he did what he did in an understanding way for George. He would need to put himself in George's shoes as the child. Even then he would need to be prepared for his son's rejection of him, given George's way of never confiding or sharing problems.

Maybe he did try to reconcile with his son, or maybe he had the same personality as George, so it was impossible. Maybe he had an immaturity that would cause him to shy away from confrontation, and have an inability to take adult responsibility in an emotional situation. George carried this anger towards his father all of his life, as he never spoke to him again, or his brother.

A Secret Tragedy

When they had to move from York House to Friar Street, we hear what a shock it was for Mary's family. George was unable to share his problems, ('My father would never confide in others, or talk about his problems,') and had kept the whole situation to himself. Keeping a silence can be to protect other people from the negative circumstances, but it can mean a shock is suffered eventually.

We don't know exactly how George felt but we know he withdrew into himself. He may have felt he was a failure, losing his house and his business, feeling responsible for the men losing their jobs. Feelings of failure and guilt would need to be visually 'handed back' to the right person, in this case the person who commissioned the building of the houses, knowing he wouldn't be able to pay. The situation is circumstance. If George had known the circumstances he would not have agreed to build the houses, but he didn't know. He would need to look at the situation in reality.

Getting help by sharing a problem, apart from benefiting the self psychologically, means that the situation has a chance to move forward, with more options. Kept inside, the problem can often go nowhere, and can stagnate.

By a twist of fate the Friar Street house is the same one George was brought up in, where his beloved mother had died and from where he had run away from an unbearable situation of grief and anger. Because he has suppressed them, these feelings would have been triggered again by being in this same house all those years later. Mary says her father became 'even more remote'.

Clearly this tragic incident affected the whole family. We hear how Ellen would retreat to her tiny plot of flowers, which she created for herself as an escape from the house, and how the children sadly missed their wonderful play area. There is now more feeling for George to carry, watching how his family is affected, and coping with the stigma of losing their large house and business, his men now unemployed. 'Looking back I think he may have been depressed,' says Mary. It is certainly possible that George did suffer from depression; he suppressed feelings, which can be a major cause. Showing his great inner strength, he built up a new business to an extent that they were able to move again within two or three years.

Symptoms of depression include lack of motivation, low energy levels, sleep problems – talking to people can become too much. In some cases there is the inability to look after the self, and people will often stop washing themselves, even stop eating or have no desire to eat. Diet can play a part too as being deprived of a healthy diet can upset the balance and help to contribute to low mood. Some people when in low mood can eat to excess, which is not healthy for the body and can lead to other physical problems, as well as making the self feel worse for behaving in this negative way. However, people who have a big inner strength can go on shouldering negative feelings for a very long time before an eventual build-up becomes a depression.

George may or may not be suffering from depression but his behaviour does demonstrate stress. We hear of irritability, being short with people, and mood changes. 'No talking was allowed and he must have had a strong influence on all of us as we kept silent. Sometimes we were wary of him, as he could suddenly be irritable and short with us, other times he would be jokey and funny, but you never knew how it was going to be,' says Mary. This behaviour demonstrates not only stress for George, but also stress for those around him. 'You never knew how it was going to be' means the people around can eventually be treading on eggshells. His family are being careful, not sure what to expect or when. They are also experiencing him becoming remote from them all. George is now carrying a lot of feelings that he is not discharging, and over time these have built up.

George's behaviour will affect the relationship he has with his children, but it will also be badly affecting the relationship between husband and wife.

Relationship Connection

'I don't know how men and women ever manage to live together,' said a colleague of mine who regularly works with couples. 'They are different species!' If we isolate ourselves as a couple, life can very often prove difficult with the male and female needs, and problems can occur within the relationship. Hopefully we can lead healthy lives by also having interaction with others: friends, colleagues and acquaintances. One of the differences between men and women is the way they connect in a marriage or sexual partnership. Women can experience more connection through shared emotion, and men can experience more connection through physical intimacy. This is of course a general theory but it can lead to misunderstandings. If a woman is approached by her partner for physical intimacy when there is no intimate connection through shared emotional relating, she can think 'All he wants is sex, he doesn't care about me,' so she doesn't know that he is opposite from her, and needs the sex to feel the connection. Of course men need emotional relating too, but if they have had difficulties opening up through life experiences or role models, emotional relating can easily become a problem, as it can for women, too.

Physical intimacy is generally an important component for men. Why are nearly all the top-shelf mags aimed at men? If there was a market for women getting pleasure from looking at pictures of naked men, then you can bet they would certainly be there in equal numbers. Look at the sex site statistics. Those 'hook up' sites where sex is on the menu, as opposed to dating sites, have thousands more men than women subscribed. Remember again this is all general; sex drives vary, not everyone is the same, and the important thing is to be happy. It doesn't matter how much sex you have, whether it's daily, weekly, monthly or yearly, if it's right for you, it's right. If you don't have a partner, you can still be having sex. I remember when I was studying towards my degree, and Maslow's 'Hierarchy of Needs' chart came up. 'You can see a man designed this!' said one female member of the class. 'Look at sex here – it's one of the basic needs and it's telling us we can't progress if we are not getting that!'

'Well, that rules me out,' someone else said. 'I don't even have a partner at the moment!' Then the tutor explained that having sex doesn't mean having a partner. We can see to our basic sexual needs by fantasy and masturbation, to name but two common ways. 'Better get the vibrator out again when I get home!' said another. 'As long as it feels right for you, that's all that matters,' said the tutor, 'and if not having sex at all feels good, then that's right too.'

Ellen, Mary's mother, is not getting the emotional connection she needs with her husband George. Non-communication and complete lack of emotional intimacy can affect their sex life as she will feel remote from him, which means George is going to be unhappy too, so there is the frustration of no connection for both of them.

'I had been married for a year and I knew I had made a mistake,' said Ellen. Living with George would have revealed to Ellen the full extent of how he dealt with intimate relating, and we can see he couldn't cope with it. He kept his feelings and troubles to himself, and could have mood changes. Having returned from the Great War there would have been more build-up from the original anger and grief he carried towards his father, and his mother's death. We hear how he can be impatient and difficult. In severe moments it is possible for this behaviour to become aggressive, but we do not hear any evidence of aggression here.

How did Ellen cope with this? It seems there were constant visitors, other family and friends, which would have helped to an extent, but we see a reference to her confiding in her child Mary. This can be unhealthy, as the child can feel burdened with the adult's problems, which they are not mature enough to handle, and also the child can be discouraged from sharing their own problems for fear of further burdening the mother. However it is eventually the youngest child, Harry, who is the chosen one for this role. Harry was sent to school a lot later than his brothers and sisters, who all started at three, but Harry was nearly six. 'I liked having him at home with me, I didn't want him to go.' Even if she hadn't said this to Harry he would have picked it up by sensing and feeling, as children do. The dilemma for him would have started at this very young age: the conflict of the need to go out into the world versus the needs of his mother. 'I made my life in my children' is going to have big consequences – we will read more about Harry in The Daughter's Story.

Mary and Frank

We hear about Mary's personality as being quiet and serious when she was a child. She often liked to be by herself, she tells us, shutting herself away with the books, to such an extent that a worried mother comes looking for her. In her wartime training when her friend Vicky is moved to a large army camp, Mary says 'I was glad it wasn't me,' further confirming this need for more quiet and space.

I rarely use the words introvert and extrovert in my work, as first of all I don't really like labels, but secondly there can be a lot of different interpretations as to what these terms mean. Many people I have come across regard introvert as a negative thing, and some have expressed feeling inadequate when in the company of what they call an extrovert.

Introverts thrive on being alone, and although they need people too, they need to recharge themselves in this way and too much of being with others can start to feel draining. Extroverts thrive on being with others and generally would prefer this to being alone, and although being alone is fine too, they eventually seek out more company. Many people are never completely one or the other, but will be somewhere on the spectrum depending on environment and parts of personality. However, we can be more strongly disposed to one than the other. Mary presents as a strong introvert, and meets Frank who comes across with a strong leaning towards extrovert. The introvert personality can become withdrawn, not because of stress or depression, but because they are trying to get the solace they need in an environment that is a social one, or because they are not enabling themselves to have the solace at all, so eventually their psyche is arranging it for them.

This is the same as thinking time. We all need thinking time for our brain to sort out our thoughts and any events of the day, and if our daily lives are completely full of mental stimulation, we can find ourselves unable to get to sleep at night, even though we feel really tired. Our psyche is seeing the opportunity for, and arranging, our thinking time.

It needs to be said that being withdrawn is not always about personality. If a person has been brought up in an environment where to be themselves or to disclose and express themselves has been met with ridicule or other forms of abuse, he or she can quickly learn to withdraw within themselves for protection. We don't hear this happening for Mary. She relates to her father as she helps him in the family business; 'I would help stick the stamps on the men's work cards and sometimes was allowed to put the wages in the envelopes.' She is the confidante of her mother and she would happily 'try out my cooking skills on the rest of the family as she had taught me, often taking the big yellow mixing bowl up to the bedroom where she lay, to ask her about a consistency of this or that.' She talks fondly of her family, 'I never resented my brothers and sisters... we were always happy together as a family,' and she expresses much disappointment when her father is not allowed leave from the army to give her away at her wedding.

Mary describes herself as quiet and serious, while Frank is described as talkative and loves to be in a party crowd. 'We were complete opposites,' states Mary. Demonstrating the opposite poles of attraction, these two have a strong chance of succeeding in a good relationship as Frank loves to talk and Mary, being quiet and serious, shunning larger gatherings, will be content to listen. So, as long as Frank can communicate and socialise with others too, they could complement each other in this way. They spend time together and discover they have interests in common, the love of visiting historical places and bike riding, a love of classical music and going to concerts. The sharing of activities carries on after they are married. It is important for future happiness that we have some things – or at least one thing – in common with a person we are choosing to spend our lives with. After all, we wouldn't choose to be with a person we had nothing in common with given a theoretical choice, as that could prove very boring and unfulfilling, resulting in never spending time together.

Mary has been brought up in an environment where her father is described as withdrawn and doesn't share his feelings or problems with anyone. Mary's mother Ellen previously described her mother as withdrawn, so this trait in George would have been familiar to Ellen and she may not have felt it as negative at the start of their relationship, even if she was aware of it, but as a familiar, comfortable place to be.

We hear very early on how Mary, at three years old, deals with her distress at being kept apart from her mother when her brother was born, and how the chocolate crushed in her little hand was where all her feeling and emotions were expressed. As she sat on the swing and her father was digging nearby, why did she not run to him in tears, receive the cuddles and warmth she craved and missed from her mother? Because she had already learned that her father didn't do these things. He was kind but could be impatient and irritable, and most of all he gave the example that you didn't talk about how you felt or show that you were upset. Mary is already experiencing a role model, teaching her to deal with negative feelings by hiding them away and suppressing them. Put this with her natural quietness and seriousness, and we are hearing about someone who eventually could also be withdrawn.

Mary, like her mother, does not play in the street with other children. She is told not to go into certain streets, or play with children in certain streets, and how poor children are 'rough'. She explains this by saying 'I don't suppose we needed to,' as there are four of them and constant visitors, and then later 'the meadows became our playground.' We may be looking at Ellen parenting in the same way that she was brought up, but we do not hear that Ellen is the same personality as her mother. We hear how she had time for all of her children and listened to their problems, how the house seemed always to have visitors including 'cockney' Uncle Charlie. George is portrayed as demanding certain behaviours from the children when they are out as a family, and there is no talking allowed at the meal table. Forbidding the children to talk to other children in certain streets or play in the street could be an extension of these behaviour demands from George, which again is a familiar trait for Ellen, as it is one her mother displayed.

Learned parenting often occurs without people considering what they are doing. Other personalities make conscious choices to never repeat what the parent did, and sometimes go to the complete opposite end of the spectrum. 'It matters what other people think' can be adopted by all sorts of different personalities. If it has been strong in the childhood upbringing it can be adopted, and very often it is just 'permission' needed to do it one's own way.

We are going to hear more about the two personalities of Frank and Mary, but first of all we are going to find out more about Frank and where he came from in 'The Father's Story'.

The Father's Story (Frank)

A London Childhood

Peckham Rye in South London is where I began life. The family had lived in this area of South London for generations, originating in the alleys around the docks, north of the Thames, and then moving across the river to Rotherhithe. It wasn't until my father bought his own house that we left South London and moved further south to Surrey, where the air was cleaner.

My father was one of eleven children and my mother was one of eight, although two babies had died.

When my mother was pregnant with me she fell victim to the terrible Spanish flu, the global disaster at the time of the Great War that killed more people than the war itself; almost 40 million died in the epidemic. She had managed to give birth to me but was far too ill to look after a new baby – luckily with our very large family it wasn't a problem. My grandmother had died eight years earlier at forty-three, and the eldest daughter, Florrie, sixteen, had then taken over as housekeeper and also mother to the youngest, Rene, who had only been eight. Now Rene was sixteen, and she took over most of the caring of me. My mother was not well enough to have much to do with me until I was six months old. She was lucky to be alive. All the brothers and sisters of both my parents lived within a three-mile radius of us. Most of their houses are now gone, as Peckham and the surrounding area suffered the worst bombing by Hitler in 1940.

My grandfather's house in Chadwick Road is still there, where we were living with him and two of my mother's brothers. By the time I was three, Rene and Florrie had married and left, but we continued to live in the house, as Granddad said he still needed a housekeeper, so my mother took over that role.

My grandfather was a very successful travelling salesman so he was frequently away for periods of time, and his sons Vic and Archie were still living with us, both in their twenties. Uncle Vic would do Granddad's paperwork, and sometimes would take various items like brooms and brushes from Granddad's stock and go around the local streets knocking on doors to try and sell them. Granddad travelled in 'household provisions' and my earliest memory is of rolling large Mansion House floor polish tins across the floor.

Uncle Archie suffered from epilepsy before there was any medication. 'That's Archie, he's the epileptic,' I heard said many times. Everyone loved Archie and it was understood he needed 'looking after'.

It suited my father that we continued to live there with Granddad, as my father's ambition was to save for and eventually own his own house. I was hardly aware of my father at that time as he worked from early morning until late at night as a post office telephone engineer, striving to accumulate enough money for home ownership. It took him eleven years, then we finally moved out of London to Surrey.

My mother's relationship with her mother-in-law was not a happy one. My father's mother was very domineering and was 'not a nice person', they said. All her children had left home as soon as possible. One of them, Lily, was rescued by her boyfriend and my father, escaping down a ladder never to return, after being regularly locked in a bedroom by her mother.

My father would take me to visit this grandmother without my mother, as Grandmother was so horrible to her. She would greet me with 'Aahh! My Frankie!' and then proceed with exaggerated sympathy, telling me my mother had no idea how to look after me properly, and how I was such a 'poor little boy'. The visits were a sense of duty and did not last long before my father stopped them all together. Her husband, my other granddad, I don't remember at all. Apparently he would either be working as many hours as he could (he was also a telephone engineer) or was in the pub, to keep out of his wife's way. This grandmother of mine was married at nineteen and gave birth to my father within five months of the marriage. She then went on to have ten more children – the last one was born when my grandmother was forty-seven. This last child was five years younger than me. We saw a lot of these aunts and uncles of mine, and I enjoyed some very good times.

When I think of those first eleven years of my childhood, it astonishes me now in the light of modern accommodation standards how we all managed, although millions of families lived in similar or much worse conditions. It was a two-up, three-down house with an outside toilet and no bathroom. There was me and later my sister Emily, both sharing one bedroom with our parents, and then Granddad with Uncle Vic and Uncle Archie sharing the other bedroom. Washing facilities were the kitchen sink, and a large zinc bath hanging outside on a nail would be dragged in periodically for baths, the water being heated in a 'wash copper' which had a cast iron drum inside for the water and an exterior of stone. Originally a fire had been lit underneath to heat the water, but now there was gas.

My memory of my sister Emily being born when I was four was a wooden cot made by my father, covered in pink and white material, with a canopy of profuse pink bows. I had never seen anything so fairy-like, and this made the contents (my sister) seem more acceptable.

I was very happy during these years, despite the overcrowded house. My mother and father's many brothers and sisters lived nearby, and we would have 'get-togethers', every house having a piano, which both my parents played, and they would be in demand for their fast duets together. We would all sing to the piano; 'My Old Man Said Follow The Van', 'Where Did You Get That Hat?' and 'My Old Dutch' were just a few of the many favourites. Sometimes Uncle Vic would do magic tricks, and one Christmas another of the uncles invented an act where I was his ventriloquist's dummy. It provided a lot of laughter.

Christmas was one long marathon party. It would start on

Christmas Eve with everyone bringing dishes of food to the house for Christmas Day, and also mysterious wrapped parcels. An hour before bedtime, Uncle Vic would take Emily and I to the market which was open very late, with all the stalls lit by naked flares, and buy us each a bag of sweets and a small toy, which we believed came from Father Christmas. We were very lucky as with so many uncles and aunts, we had lots of presents. One year I received a toy mechanical gramophone with several small records. I played the records over and over again, which must have been as maddening to the relations as a drum and trumpet were another year. Then there was the electric train set which in contrast seemed to fascinate all the uncles even more than myself. The Christmas meals were huge: dinner with the turkey and trimmings, Christmas pudding and mince pies, and then the tea with jelly, tinned fruit, blanc-mange, chocolate roll, Dundee cake and iced Christmas cake. Supper would be served some time after midnight, comprising of cold beef, ham, beetroot, bubble and squeak, and sausage rolls. Lemonade and ginger beer would be for us children, and there were plenty of chocolates, nuts, dates, Turkish delight, apples and oranges in dishes around the house. There was continuous piano playing, as all the aunts played, as well as my mother and father. Singing would sometimes be replaced by an uncle producing a new board game. Eventually, in the small hours, people would fall asleep on the various chairs and the sofa, and sometimes the floor. It was easier than walking home, and obviously the two bedrooms upstairs were already full. On Boxing Day it started all over again.

I must say I don't think Emily and I appreciated how lucky we were to have these very happy Christmases. There was much poverty in the district, and although not patently obvious to us children, a hint of it was evident in the annual pre-Christmas announcement at school. 'Poor children' were offered tickets for a free show at the Saturday morning cinema, where they received a bag of sweets, an apple and an orange. Emily and I always put our hands up for this, as there was never any check on the poverty state, and it became clear that anyone could apply as we lived in a poor district. 'You're cheating,' our mother would say. 'You're not poor,' but we went all the same.

The Tower Cinema was very close to our house, so we were allowed to go to the 'Saturday morning pictures' in the winter, and it was here I saw my first films, all silent: *The Gold Rush* with Charlie Chaplain, Harold Lloyd comedies, and then my first talking picture came: *Sonny Boy* with Al Jolson.

Both my parents were talented pianists; they had originally met at a party and hit it off immediately, playing duets together. They were then in demand at many parties in the area. I was nine and Emily was six when we started lessons. Each lesson terminated with a stern instruction to practice regularly. Emily was more receptive than me and perhaps more dutiful. There were too many distractions for me to concentrate. In the street outside the front window were continuous street games. Wooden hoop rolling, hopscotch, fivestones, marbles, conkers, whip tops, cigarette card flicking, roller skating, and wheeled ball bearing box carts were the most popular games, and it was where I spent all my time.

Catching a tram to Abbey Wood was for Saturdays, and several of us boys would ride out together and spend the day tree-climbing and camp-building. Abbey Wood is now of course a housing district and I think the woods have disappeared. There was also Forest Hill with a very steep gully from top to bottom, in which we would slide continuously down on pieces of old wood or anything else we could find. On the way to the hill we would pass houses with gardens containing fruit trees, some having glass fragments set in concrete on the top of the walls. Whilst this would usually be very effective to deter people from climbing over the wall, for us boys it provided a challenge, an obstacle to be overcome. This activity, known as 'scrumping', meant that we would arrive home with various handfuls of fruit. Even when caught by a policeman, if we failed to evade his clutches (as sometimes occurred) a clip round the ear was regarded by all as a fair outcome.

Our street games were safe and uninterrupted as the car was rarely seen in my small world. The baker's delivery cart complete with horse, the rag 'n' bone man, and occasionally a tricycle with a large box on the front selling ice cream was all the traffic we saw in our street.

On the main road there were two bus companies, The General Bus Company and Thomas Tillings Ltd. so there was fierce competition. Every bus would stop anywhere on the route to pick up or alight passengers, as not to do so meant loss of business.

Sometimes we had a holiday and would travel all the way to Clacton by paddle steamer from Tower Pier near Tower Bridge on the Thames. Watching the giant pistons and huge paddle wheels revolving in the water was a huge thrill for me. However, the Clacton holidays were continual sufferings of agony for me from a very early age. My father held the view that the most effective method of learning to swim was to be suddenly dropped into the deep water. Enforced seaside boat trips had me cowering and weeping in the bottom of the boat. Eventually, when I reached fourteen, I managed to overcome my phobia of the water and learned to swim by trial and error at school where, suspended in the water in a canvas strap on a long bamboo pole, the teacher would shout instructions. I also gained a keen appetite for the buns and cakes that were to follow which my mother would sympathetically pack up for me in encouragement.

What I did find fascinating at Clacton was a small 'aeroplane field' which we walked through to get to the beach. Alan Cobham, who was to become holder of the world land speed record in his Sunbeam, the first car to reach 200 miles an hour, provided short flights in his single engine bi-plane. The cost was five shillings, a lot of money, but I was very content to just watch the taking off, the flying, and the landing, sitting for hours on the field edge, while the family was entrenched in deckchairs on the beach.

As soon as I came home from school, if Granddad was at home and not away working I would be required to go to the off-licence for a bottle of Whitbread's Pale Ale and then to the butcher's shop for a meat chop or half a pound of rump steak. The errand would be Monday to Saturday, which meant six days a week, every day taking the empty beer bottle back for which there was a penny on 'returns'.

This was my reward for going and it meant sixpence a week for me, regarded as quite an immense sum for a child. Another errand was transporting a parcel of my mother's washing on a home-made ball bearing scooter (they were all the rage with my friends) to my aunty's house, to be included with hers to be sent to the laundry. The outward journey of around two miles was difficult, trying to balance the parcel and steer at the same time, but the return journey was fast and fun. I was paid a 'threp'ny bit' for this errand (three pennies). As was common in those days, a lot of this money was spent on sweets; gobstoppers, jelly babies, sherbert dabs, liquorice allsorts, coconut squares, Pontefract cakes, and boiled sweets of every flavour and colour. No wonder we had to visit the dentist and have treatment so often. The visits filled me with dread. All fillings and extractions were done with an anaesthetic called 'gas'. A gas mask was put on the nose causing a fearful fight for breath before the anaesthetic took effect. I remember the sight of blood and aching soreness afterwards as a terrifying experience at eight years old.

The mention of gas always reminds me of my father who suffered poisonous gas attacks in the Great War. I remember a set of books at one of my friend's houses really making an impression on me, particularly the illustrations, which were informative, realistic and sometimes horrifyingly tragic about the First World War. It was my first realisation of the scale and intensity of the human slaughter involved. Yet my father, who served in the trenches and experienced the dreadful conditions of service throughout that war, never once referred to the subject, nor did we ever discuss it in his lifetime.

I was eight years old when I discovered I was very good at sport. The annual school sports day saw me entered for the 100 yards sprint, the 220 yards, the egg and spoon and the potato race. My father was suddenly very interested as he was a keen sportsman, playing in the cricket and football teams where he worked at the GPO. He offered me lots of advice about each race, and I was very nervous and a bit bewildered as I had never done anything like this before. To my great surprise and my parents' delight, I won every race and received a cricket bat as a prize. After that my father found out which races won the most points so making it more likely to win the championship cup, and told me to enter for these races. I became quite keen after my first success and started 'training' with a friend, running 'round the block' each evening. The following year I continued my success by winning everything I entered for and won the trophy cup. The prize for each race was a cricket bat and as I had already won one of these the previous year and didn't really need another half dozen, my father stepped in and made sure all the runners-up received them. I repeated this the next year too, and everyone must have breathed a sigh of relief when we finally moved away to Surrey and I left the school.

When we moved to Surrey, Uncle Vic asked if he could come with us. My father said he could if he got a 'proper job'. Vic had been doing my grandfather's paperwork and selling things door-to-door. My father was expecting him to pay regular rent as money was tight with a growing family, my father having managed at last to buy his own house. Uncle Vic then immediately got a job as a postman and continued in this job for the rest of his working life. My father had an ongoing problem with Vic though, as after he had a bath (we now had a proper bathroom) Vic would walk around the house stark naked, 'drying naturally' he would say, which was 'healthier'. If my father was there when this happened, Vic would get banished back to the bedroom or the bathroom with a cry of 'For goodness sake, Vic, get some clothes on!' If there had been a naturist club in the area I'm sure Vic would have joined it. Eventually, Uncle Vic moved out to his own little rented house not far away, where he continued to be very much part of the family.

Eventually leaving school at fourteen, my father and uncle, both working for the GPO, managed to get me a job as an indoor messenger boy in the London telegraph head office. After a while I was accepted for training as a post office counter clerk in Leicester Square post office. I was the fourth generation to work for the GPO in our family. The first was my great grandfather, who had been a stoker and then a steam engine operator in the post office telegraph steam engine room in the 1800s (the telegraph equipment was driven by steam), and then my grandfather and my father, who were both post office telephone engineers.

Under The Hood Part 3

Frank's family is a large, extended one, very physically close, as not only are they all living within the same neighbourhood but a lot of them are living in the same house. He was allowed much freedom as a child, which he enjoyed immensely and we see his social side as he loves the family gatherings and the playing outside whenever he can. Frank's strong humanitarian side comes across in the way he reminisces about the living standards of the time, the poor children of the district, and his description of the events of World War One as 'horrifyingly tragic'.

There is not the stigma of a poor divide here, being a much freer approach. They live in a 'poor district', which becomes apparent to him at school with the free cinema at Christmas. There is no 'keeping up appearances' by staying away from the poor streets, as we hear about in the Suffolk environment.

Frank's Question

Frank describes a very secure environment, and the benefits of an extended family can clearly be seen. The near death and subsequent inability of Frank's mother to care for him as a newborn is not seen as a problem, as there are many family members to help, and Rene becomes his surrogate mum.

Frank's memory of his father as a 'remote figure' was far less of a problem as a small child than it could have been, as he has so many other adults to relate to, including two uncles and a grandfather who live in the same house as himself. However, this security is blighted by Frank's father's attitude to child rearing. We get two examples: continually forcing him as a small child in a very cruel way to learn to swim, and enforced boat trips resulting in Frank weeping in the bottom of the boat. Frank calls it his 'continual sufferings of agony', and he suffered from a very early age. We see a father's cruel behavior devoid of all human feeling and empathy. Why?

There are several possible reasons why Frank's father adopted this behaviour.

First, it could have been a fear of how his son was growing up. This can stem from an inadequacy in the father as he feels he needs his son to be a good reflection on himself. 'If my son is a certain person then I will be regarded well. If my son is not a certain person then I will be not be regarded well.' A son who is sensitive and a little nervous could be in danger of becoming a victim here; 'I was very nervous and a bit bewildered,' says Frank about the school sports day, for example. With the old negative attitude of what makes a man, which did not include any so-called feminine traits of sensitivity, a father could fear his son is in danger of not becoming 'a proper man', and not knowing what to do about this, in his ignorance and fear, could try to force a change, trying to 'toughen him up' or 'make more of a man of him'. This cruel, insensitive behaviour would only have served to damage the relationship between father and son, as well as damaging Frank psychologically. But Frank was able to overcome what he called his 'phobia', and learns to swim at school, where a sympathetic and understanding teacher provides the right environment. Frank eventually proved his natural ability for being very good at all physical sports, which was something he did have in common with his father.

We know now of course that both men and women are people with sensitivities and emotions. The old idea in our society of 'men don't cry', 'it isn't manly to cry' was potentially very damaging. Crying is a healthy release of feelings, and in the previous story,

George, who needed to grieve, may have suffered from this belief, commonly held at that time.

Second, an upbringing in an abusive household can cause learned behaviour to abuse. The only thing we know about Frank's father's upbringing is that he had an abusive mother. Frank heard that his grandmother was 'not a nice person', and where his mother was concerned 'was so horrible to her'. All the children left home as soon as they could we are told, and the tale of Lily escaping down a ladder from her locked bedroom and never returning tells us what an unbearable situation it must have been. Little Frank's visits to his grandmother were eventually stopped by his father, and Frank has no memory of the grandfather as he was 'working as many hours as he could, or was in the pub, to keep out of his wife's way.' The father in this abusive household we hear was ineffective; the male role model would have been remote and not a strong one. Cutting off from painful feelings as a child can result in an inability to feel as an adult, so empathy can be lost.

We have to remember that a childhood in an abusive family does not automatically produce an abusive adult. It depends on the personality as to how it manifests. Some people will go completely the opposite way and be too 'soft', to the extent that their children do not have the containing boundaries they need for security. Some people bring their children up in very loving secure environments, remembering their own suffering. Abusive personalities are very often weak personalities who cannot look at their own behaviour very well, and will often deny it. Because they are unable to acknowledge what they do, they also are never able to change. Sometimes they do acknowledge it but are stuck in a 'martyr' position, always apologising but never taking any responsibility to try and do it differently, so the suffering of others continues.

Third, an emotional immaturity can cause childish feelings and behaviour to surface in an adult in certain situations. Jealousy of the child's relationship with his or her mother can surface. It is a sad situation as the father is as important to the child as the mother, and the role can be different. The father feels left out, he is not getting the mother's attention as before, and instead of creating his own role and building a relationship with his child, enabling himself and his wife to enjoy their child together, he turns into a bullying big brother.

Frank had other positive male role models and relationships with his many uncles, whom he saw a lot of, living with two of them, and describes this time as a very happy one. It would seem that Frank's father's absence from home ('I was hardly aware of my father at that time') which lasted eleven years as he worked as many hours as he could saving for their own home, was a blessing. It was at family holiday times that the negative situations would have had a good opportunity to surface.

Perversion?

Was Vic's eventual behaviour of walking around the house naked after a bath and 'drying naturally' a perversion? Several people have commented on this. The behaviour would be more normal now for some people as we live in a freer and more relaxed time.

Vic presents as an eccentric of the times. This behaviour only occurred when the family moved to a house with a bathroom. Previously the overcrowded and communal conditions of the family kitchen would have given more opportunity for exposure. There are no previous incidents mentioned and no other similar incidents either, where we could suspect any damaging behaviour occurring. The children lived with Vic for nearly the whole of their childhoods and after that he was only 'down the road and still very much part of the family.'

Behaviour by predatory paedophiles and dangerous exhibitionists is normally done in secret, the perpetrator taking great care that no adult will ever find out. Great guilt can be carried, not only by the victim, but also by the parent when they eventually find out what was happening. 'Why didn't I see it? I should have known!' is a common reaction. The perpetrator however knows their behaviour is wrong and will go to all lengths to make sure they are not found out. Selfish traits and immaturity can result in them giving in to their own desires and the damage is caused. These days the word 'paedophile' can be taken to mean someone who abuses children, but the meaning is someone who is sexually attracted to children. There are people who are sexually attracted to children who would never act on it. Caring people who take responsibility for their actions, and recognise the harm it can do, will make sure they are never in a situation where this could happen. It is clear it isn't just the children Vic does this in front of, as Frank's father soon tells him to cover up when he happens to be there. It doesn't sound like it changes the behaviour, as Frank's father had a problem with it happening recurrently. Vic may have a selfish trait in that he does what he wants to do regardless, or maybe he has a rebellious streak. The behaviour seems strange or unusual to the family, which is what eccentric behaviour is. He probably would have been very happy as a naturist.

Something Wrong?

This is a lovely account of a London pre-war childhood, a way of life that has now disappeared. It is however different from the previous two stories. It gives lots of information about events and things within those events, often in a lot of detail. It tells us who all the people are, but it doesn't tell us about the people themselves, what they were like, apart from the holiday incidents with his father. We don't hear what Frank's mother is like as a person, or any of the aunts and uncles, or how Frank feels towards any of them.

Was he close to his mother? Or any of his aunts or uncles? Or his granddad? What were they like as people? We don't know.

There is a tragic story that Frank's daughter Jilly will tell us in The Daughter's Story, involving Frank's sister Emily when they were both children, but Frank doesn't even mention it. 'Well, this is a man writing and the other two stories are written by women,' said a friend, which I found to be rather sexist. It is true that men and women's brains can work differently when it comes to emotional situations, or a crisis. The differences are general, and there will be exceptions and a spectrum of behaviour depending on the person. Women can stay with the feelings, whilst men can feel at first, and then have the ability to quickly switch to the problem-solving part of the brain. Of course males do feel deep emotion, and male writers express this in a beautiful way. I gave the story to my son to read. 'It's very factual,' was his comment.

Is Frank another person like George who has difficulty with emotion, and expressing feelings? We find out in the next story as the answer lies with Frank's daughter Jilly, as she tells The Daughter's Story, with many other revelations regarding all three generations.

The Daughter's Story (Jilly)

Childhood

Most of my earliest memories are with my grandmothers. I was very close to both of them, my mother Mary being a quiet and withdrawn person. I never quite forgave her for calling me 'Jillian' and not spelling it right. I was constantly having to tell people how to spell it, as everyone thought it was Gillian. The rest of the family however, including my father, always called me Jilly so that's who I have always been to most people. One of my early memories of my mother is when I was about six years old, running through the kitchen towards the garden on a warm sunny day. Suddenly I am stopped in my tracks by the sight of my mother bent over the kitchen sink, a mountain of washing-up on the draining board. As I look at her bent back, a feeling of sadness comes over me. I want to help her, to offer to do some dish drying, but another part of me is longing to join the playing children in the garden. 'I wish she would just ask me!' I remember thinking. 'And then I would!' I hung around for probably a few seconds and nothing happened, nothing came from the growing pile of plates and saucepans. Then the little child took over, the strongest feeling became paramount, and I skipped out into the sunshine.

Another much earlier memory is of me sitting on a draining board. It was at my Nanna's house in Surrey, having been put there by my mother. I was dripping wet from a heavy rain shower, we had both run home, me being dragged along laughing. It was in this same kitchen with its slippery rush mat where I was playing on the floor, when a saucepan descended onto me from the cooker above. The contents were probably not absolutely boiling as I have no scars, but there was a lot of screaming and I'm sitting in an armchair, my mother bathing my face with cotton wool and some sort of liquid in a white pudding basin. Then I am in the back of a neighbour's car, tearfully clinging to my mother. 'Would she like to sit in the front with me?' he said, kind words well meant. 'No! I don't want to, it hurts, I want Mummy!' was inside my head. 'No,' said a little pathetic voice and I clung harder to my mother. 'I think she'd rather sit with me,' said my mother. Then the white masks looming over me, the funny smell, the screaming coming from me, and my mother attempting to comfort me, trying to read me my favourite book.

'She looks like a nun!' said my father that evening. I was bandaged all around my head and face and down both arms. I have a memory of my mother refusing to show me a mirror. 'You were scalded,' said Nanna.

I loved my Nanna; she was such a jolly person, always having time for me when we visited, even after her working day in London where she was head of a typing pool. She would teach me 'Jesus Bids Us Shine' (she was a staunch Methodist) and we would sing it together, as well as 'Daisy Daisy Give Me Your Answer Do', and 'She Was a Dear Little Dicky Bird'. My Aunty Emily, who lived with Nanna, was my father's sister and was blind. When I was very small I was rather wary of her. She would sit in her chair all day and when I spoke to her she always said 'I beg your pardon?' She couldn't understand what I said, so we never had a conversation, as I soon gave up. In later years I realised she had been ill as it was only three years later that she died of kidney failure, but I hadn't known this at the time.

Nanna eventually told me the story when I was about eight years old, of how tragedy had struck the family. Emily was running home from school with a friend along one of the unmade roads, where houses were still being built, and their legs became intertwined and Emily fell and forcefully hit her head. Her friend brought her home and from that moment on she was blind. She was nine years old.

The hospital couldn't help and her father paid for Harley Street doctors. They said she had a tumour on the brain, but no operations or scans were available in those days. Then she started having fits. Her father was heartbroken over it. 'I can cope with blindness but I can't cope with the fits,' he said, according to Nanna. She reckoned he never got over it and as the years went by he seemed to become more and more tired and withdrawn until he died at the age of forty-seven. Later my father told me it was the gas in the Great War that had caused the cancer, but this was Nanna's story. 'He died of a broken heart,' she said. Of course they were all used to Archie with the fits, and it was never known if the fall had caused the onset of the fits or whether it was unrelated and the fits were part of a hereditary pattern. In those days the medication had side effects on the kidneys. Emily died of kidney failure at thirty-three.

I was living with my parents in a middle-class suburb of North London, a 1930s house with little stained glass windows. 'Wow, Mum, it's posh!' said my youngest daughter over forty years later, as we walked down the hill from the Tube station, along the wide, tree-lined avenues, a historical visit to the past. I had never thought of it like that. Something you've known forever can be taken for granted. It just *is,* like my grandmother's parents never living together.

There were many families with children in the neighbourhood, and my childhood was a very happy one. Being allowed to 'play out' constantly, I was always either in someone else's house, in the park on the swings, or climbing trees and building camps on the wasteland. It was heartbreaking when they built on that wasteland. I was a teenager by then but my memories seemed violated.

My father Frank seemed to be mainly at home at weekends, when he would spend his time digging and generally tending our very long back garden. On weekdays I would catch a fleeting glimpse as he arrived home from the London office, ate his dinner extremely quickly, which had been saved for him, to hurry out again for a council meeting. He had managed to get himself elected as an independent councillor, and had become chairman of the housing committee. Sometimes I would be hovering near when he was surrounded with the many letters he received from people in trouble, about damp conditions, harassment, homelessness, or rent they couldn't pay. He genuinely wanted to and tried to help these people. He had a strong humanitarian side, which I inherited from him – I trained as a Samaritan at the age of twenty-five, after seeing a poster on the train.

I also inherited my father's love and talent for sport. He would always take the time off work to attend a sports day, as I would be active in the school sports, the Brownie sports, and representing the school at the district sports. He would cheer me on loudly with my running both long distance and sprint, and stand patiently watching the high jump. I regularly won the cup, or the runners-up medal, and like him many years ago, would run 'round the block' in the evenings, getting my mother to time me with an old stop watch. This was before I had heard any stories about him doing the same when he was a young boy.

Holidays were lovely. Two weeks every year we would have a caravan or a chalet on the coast. We would spend hours on the beach, my father making us cars and boats out of sand to play in. He would take us for long walks in the countryside showing us the Saxon round towers of isolated Norfolk churches, discovering pounds of blackberries in the hedgerows, and sitting on corn bales, splitting the grain to eat.

He would always encourage me to go in the sea, accompanying me to play in the water, or later patiently be with me to encourage me in my attempts to swim in a rubber ring. When I heard his story of his horrible experience with his own father I felt very grateful towards him, and still remember his enthusiasm and great patience with me, making it all so much fun. He must have remembered his great hardship as a child.

The two loves of my life are still walking and swimming.

Another parallel with my father was the piano lesson. I also would do the bare minimum of practice, preferring to be out tree climbing, making camps, chalking hopscotch on the pavements, and the tremendously exciting pursuit of wheeling bikes to the top of one of the hills and then tearing down faster and faster, sometimes two of us on one bike, somehow managing to avoid crashing into the trees lining the avenue on the way down. These trees had a special lure in the autumn as every other one was a horse chestnut, meaning several of us would congregate around a particularly fruitful tree and throw sticks, cricket bats, and anything we could lay our hands on from the garden shed to knock those big, shiny conkers down. After a while, the person whose house we happened to be outside would decide they'd had enough and would bang angrily on the window. We would move on to another one leaving behind masses of leaves, conker cases, small branches and twigs littering the pavement. In the spring us girls would fill our school berets with the cherry blossom from the cherry trees that alternated with the horse chestnuts.

On Saturdays I was not seen at home from early morning until the end of the day, apart from a fleeting visit to ravenously gulp down dinner, which was always midday and the main meal.

My brother on the other hand would be at home with Mum and practice piano for hours on end, doing clever things like exams. Schubert's 'Musical Moments' still grates on me today after hearing it over and over for many months. I would do the minimum of piano practice and be gone, although I have always enjoyed playing the piano. My father sometimes played duets with me as a child. We had some very old sheet music, which he'd had as a child, with the mysterious name 'Diabelli' in big letters across the front. The duets of Diabelli were quite easy for me to play and sometimes Dad and me would thump them out with great gusto, getting louder and faster and laughing more and more as we finally collapsed at the end. It was Nanna, though, who I loved to hear play. Nanna and the granddad I never knew were well known in their district of South London when they were teenagers. They played many duets together and were much in demand for parties and other gatherings before the time of DJs and electronic music. Their famous duet was called 'Qui Vive', a fast piece, and when I was around and Granddad had long since died, she would play this duet by herself, improvising for both parts, very loud and fast, and I would watch spellbound. Although I had learned the piano I didn't have the application for study and practice, but also I didn't have Nanna's amazing gift for improvisation. She could hear a tune on the radio and sit down and play it, with two hands and adding her own twiddly bits. I would play Chopin, leaving out half the notes as it was hard to play, and making up my own, simple style, but Nanna loved it. 'Come on Jilly, let's have some Chopin!' she would say, and then, 'Our Jilly has such a lovely touch.' My brother Andrew, completely opposite to me, would stick stolidly at it, plodding his way through each exam, eventually achieving his music degree and becoming a teacher, but none of us had inherited Nanna's wonderful gift of spontaneous improvisation.

Chalk and cheese, that was me and my brother. I was out all the time like Dad, he was in with Mum. I remember one time when he did come out with us kids. We were at a favourite spot, a pond where we would make our way along the pond edge, holding on to the branches and bushes overhanging the waters edge, to reach a secret spot cut off by brambles and undergrowth. He got a little scared and we shouted encouragement, and then he just let go, falling backwards into the water. It was shallow but he was very wet, and we deposited him back with Mum dripping and miserable. I don't remember him coming out with us again.

Our problems started with my father when we started to talk and wanted to relate in a close way. He was very literal and also would sometimes have a defensive and sometimes attacking attitude, so problems soon arose. I remember crying myself to sleep, my mother stroking my face, but unable to deal with it, saying nothing. My brother had the same problem, and we both suffered in adulthood in certain areas. My brother to this day can have a problem relating to certain older men, and I kept quiet in groups and with certain other people, because of my experience of being talked over by my father. I eventually accepted myself and allowed myself to be totally me, after many years in various work training, some personal therapy, and with the support of some marvellous friends. It wasn't until many years later when, as a support worker during a training session, I read a list of Asperger's Syndrome symptoms, and I thought 'That's Dad!' But it wasn't heard of in those days when we were children.

It didn't help having a withdrawn mother too, of course, as this only increased the problem. 'Your children are very quiet, Mary!' said a friend of my mother who we were visiting when we were quite small. I remember the voice almost bordered on concern. Mum always worried about what other people thought, and she didn't like other people looking at her, which she thought they were even when they weren't. 'Ssshhh!' she would say, trying to curb my natural childish expression, me more than my brother as I had a lot of natural exuberance.

What with our father talking over us and our mother's discouraging expression, we actually became withdrawn ourselves, but for me it was only in certain company. I was closer to my grandmothers than my mother, and expression was encouraged with them. However the whole family completely ignored my father's behaviour, allowing everything to continue without explanation of any kind, so my brother and I believed there was something wrong with us when we couldn't relate to him. How had he managed to rise with promotion in the Civil Service and serve as an independent councillor on the housing committee? One event in memory however tells me all was not well on the work front. The housing committee finally unanimously voted him out. 'Try to be quiet, your dad's upset,' I was told one evening when I was about eleven. 'They've all been awful to him, and all those years he's put in!' My mother was shocked at the ousting, but wasn't able to consider why it had happened.

Despite my mother's problem of suppression, and my father's Asperger's, I did have normal relating with grandmothers, aunt and uncle, and later was to finally marvel at the outside world with so many people in it who wanted to relate and listen to what I had to say, and more importantly responded to it as well.

When my brother was born I was two years old and in Sudbury with my other grandmother, my mother's mother Ellen who I called Grandma. These visits then continued every year and into my teens; I would go regularly for several weeks to stay. She loved having me, saying I was 'no trouble', and it must have been a welcome respite for my mother. I loved it there, as my grandma adored children and took me everywhere with her. Looking back, I remember I never saw any other children and would be mostly in a world of old ladies or solitary play in the garden, but I was very happy.

There was Uncle Harry too, my mother's brother, who also lived there, and when not working he would take me for walks across the meadows. I have never been frightened of cows as every time we saw a herd, we would walk right through the middle of them. He would let me climb on the brick 'pill boxes' built to dissuade the Germans from sailing up the River Stour in World War Two. Sometimes he would sit me on the bridge at Sudbury station and we would watch the little 'coffee pot' engines shunting up and down. I loved my Uncle Harry, but many years later I realised that he never ever managed to leave home permanently and make a life for himself. Now and again he would take yet another job in a nearby town, living in lodgings, but after a while would return again to the family home in Sudbury. Harry was the last child to be at home and Grandma hadn't wanted him to go. 'I made my life in my children,' she would say, and this life was fast disappearing as one after another the children left to make their own lives. My Uncle Harry always had back pain, in and out of hospital, tests, support belts, traction, it was always the same in the end. 'There's nothing physically wrong,' said the various doctors and hospitals, 'it's psychological.' These days he could have had help but although psychological conditions were recognised, there wasn't much help for them then. He had a girlfriend once, I really liked her – she was good fun and I remember her taking me swimming. They became engaged but it didn't last long after that. We were told Uncle Harry had a 'nervous breakdown' and the engagement ended almost immediately. Eventually, many years later when his mother died, he had to leave the family home and bought himself a little maisonette. In and out of hospital with back pain and then depression, he was admitted to hospital one day for pain relief, contracted pneumonia and died. 'It's like you're carrying the world on your shoulders,' I exclaimed to him on a visit, shocked to see his bent frame. They never expected him to die but he was so thin, he just never had any reserves to fight it.

His brother, my Uncle Will, had married and pursued a successful career in the City as an accountant. However, we called him 'the uncle who never spoke'. Visits from him would be dreaded as we sat around trying to think of further things to say after his monosyllabic answers to our questions. 'How's Pat?' Mum would ask. 'Fine,' Will would say, then silence again, all to be repeated when I was grown up and he was visiting me and my family. Wife Pat and Will never visited together. In fact it seemed they never did anything together. I used to think, 'Well, why would she want to? He's such hard work and so boring.' 'Lizzie's the only normal one,' I once heard a family friend say, and I suppose she was. She was sweet and made me feel special, like her mother, my grandma. Aunty Lizzie married a Welshman so I didn't see her much after that, as Wales was a long way to visit and as a child we didn't have a car.

During my Sudbury visits, occasionally I would be in Granddad's carpentry workshop at the end of the road, putting the curly wood shavings on my head pretending I had curls instead of my very straight hair. I was always a little afraid of my granddad, George, as sometimes he was a bit gruff, and I was never sure whether he was in a bad mood, as other times he would make me laugh with silly jokes. There was always silence at the meal table, and my mother would tell me that he was very strict when she was a child, no talking allowed. When I was in the front room at the piano where I would spend many hours tinkering and playing about, he would suddenly come into the room and play something very loud and fast which I thought was brilliant. Then he might try to teach me something, but he had no patience with me, and would end up raising his voice, which meant I then couldn't do anything at all, and he would go away in exasperation. It did not put me off however, as his visits were rare.

Grandma took me regularly to the Methodist chapel on Sundays where I was given a sweet to suck during the sermon to 'keep me quiet'. I was taken to socials, teas, and 'bright hours' at the chapel, which I did enjoy as everyone made a lot of fuss of me. Where I lived with my mother and father was a different story. Being made to go to church every Sunday and sit through long services and very boring sermons week after week gave me a lifetime aversion to it. Protests did no good, nor shouting, nor later door slamming. I had to go and that was it. The consequence was that none of my children were christened as I told them they could make up their own minds about it when they grew up. I wanted nothing more to do with the very boring church.

My world was an idyll as a child but as I grew older, I started to see it with different eyes. I started to feel I didn't really like it there in my mother's dream neighbourhood. I realised how the people kept themselves to themselves, and there was not the friendliness of the neighbourhoods I experienced in Sudbury. People existed in their own private worlds behind the net curtains and you rarely got a glimpse. If I lifted our net curtain to view someone or something outside, I would be told to 'Put that curtain down!' The swift and loud command would be obeyed. For my mother it was perfect. Quiet and withdrawn, she liked the status of it, the safety of the middle-class Townswomen's Guild, and the 'Thursday Club' held in the church hall opposite, where I would help to put the sticky buns onto plates when it was her turn to do the 'teas', looking forward to sampling one. Eventually, I found that for me there was no warmth, no passion, no human feeling. I left as soon as I could.

Hertfordshire

Unfortunately, I did not leave home in the way I should have done. I got married too young, when I should have been exploring the world. When the babies came I loved them dearly and those times are definitely some of the happiest of my life. The mistake was marrying the wrong person, but I was in love.

My husband Carl and myself lived with our two children Tom and Mandy on a new estate in Hertfordshire; we were now moving from this very new house to a very old house, and it was an exciting time for all of us. Built as the home of a wealthy merchant in 1680, it had become part of a school many years later. It was now divided into four separate houses and we were lucky to have the middle part with the original entrance – a grand porch with pillars and seats. There was no bathroom, an outside toilet, four bedrooms, cellars, an attic, a big garden and lots of work to be done.

Some people thought we were mad to move, including my father-in-law, who couldn't understand why we would want to swap a nice new house on a new estate in good repair, for one that was over 300 years old with no inside toilet or bathroom and which had damp. It was enough to give him a heart attack, he said – and ironically he did have a heart attack, but that was many years later.

We started to enjoy our project. We managed to acquire an improvement grant, and the builders moved in. All four of us moved into one very large bedroom which housed a chemical toilet in an adjoining cupboard, as the first thing the builders did was to knock down the outside toilet, to lay foundations for the new bathroom.

This outside toilet was very interesting. It adjoined the house and was on the other side of the kitchen wall. The toilet cistern was actually in the kitchen with the chain hanging down by the side of the kitchen sink, and disappearing through the wall into the adjoining toilet outside – very sensible actually as this minimised freezing of the cistern water in the winter. The children would think it great fun to wait until someone was in the toilet and then pull the chain from inside the kitchen; the person sitting in peace on the other side of the wall would be suddenly surprised by a deluge of water below them. There was some disappointment when this feature was removed after we had lived there just a short time.

It was in this house that the experiences started; it was the day I met Annie next door that I had my first introduction to another dimension of life.

Annie was a lady in her fifties who had 'a bad heart' and lots of little bottles of pills lined up for her to take every day. Her husband Colin was working in London at that time and would catch the train every morning. Annie's house was exactly as they had bought it thirty years earlier. There was still the outside toilet and no bathroom, although there was a funny-looking bath in the corner of the kitchen with a wooden lid on it and piles of washing and other paraphernalia. The whole time we lived there I was sure no one used it. There was no damp course, and the window frames were clinging on for dear life, with no paint on them to speak of. I felt sorry for her as she was housebound, not able to walk far, and alone for most of the day.

She was standing in the garden at the little back fence waiting for the opportunity to meet and talk.

'If Colin sees what you're doing with your house, maybe he'll do ours,' she would say, beaming at me.

Years of living in these conditions, regularly watching her husband Colin reading the *Financial Times* 'to check his shares', she had not been able to persuade her husband to take on the project. Maybe they couldn't afford it, but no money had been spent on the house for comfort. Colin did do the house up eventually, but sadly she wasn't there to enjoy it.

'When my son was twelve, he said he saw a little fair-haired boy coming through the wall of his bedroom from your house,' she said. 'I've seen him too, you know.'

I was fascinated and wanted to know more. Who was this crazy woman? 'Well, these houses used to be a school,' she said. 'Sometimes I hear him.'

Having had no experience of anything like this, I went back to Carl saying 'There's a mad woman next door!'

And after recounting the story, he said, 'Don't tell the children, it might frighten them.'

Our life in the old house continued happily. The children made friends; we made friends. It was a great community in a street that was full of old houses and people who were passionate about them, like we were. Everyone was interested in what we were doing, and Carl managed to find some very old photographs at the local museum, showing the house pre-1900 before the Edwardian kitchen extensions were built and the building was all as one. A couple of men could be seen working in the garden in what looked like their Sunday best, the way they would dress in those days, and a couple of ladies at the original back door (which was now a window), in similar splendid attire of long dresses and lace caps.

We uncovered a huge inglenook fireplace in the living room, and the builders replaced the living room floor. We were walking across planks for weeks to reach the front door, a six-feet drop below to the cellar. Layers of cream gloss paint which seemed an inch thick had protected a lot of the woodwork, and the removal of numerous layers of wallpaper eventually revealed strange green walls displaying graffiti from another age.

I got to know Annie better. She would always welcome me with a cup of tea or coffee when I wanted to escape the house with the builders and the mess. We became quite close. I would sit and listen to her stories about how 'I can see pictures around people, about what has happened to them and what will happen.' 'I knew my mother was going to die a week before she did.' Annie was a psychic, and sometimes people would come in and ask her to 'do the cards'. I gradually became very interested in the whole thing, keeping an open mind. She told me one of my spirit guides was a child; she told me I had chosen my parents with the purpose of going through certain experiences; I took it all with a pinch of salt.

Later, she told me the baby I was pregnant with was a girl, and she was right.

Eventually we were all sitting in our newly refurbished kitchen, having Sunday lunch around the large, old 1940s dining table which my mother-in-law had given us, when Tom, aged eight, said, 'Edward's outside.'

Edward was Tom's latest best friend. The kitchen door was half glass, so people could clearly be seen. I looked up but saw no one. I got up and opened the door. There was no one there. I looked up the garden that had a long, straight path to the top leading to a back walkway which was also exposed, but no one was there.

'He *was* there,' Tom insisted, 'he walked *that* way,' pointing past the kitchen door towards the house wall.

I looked – there was nowhere to go, the path ended at the house and Tom was pointing towards a window. Then it suddenly dawned on me.

I remembered the very old photographs and the ladies standing at the door in their lace caps. This was the spot, the window used to be the old door, before the extensions were built, and Edward was a little boy with very fair hair.

A few months later I was cooking in the kitchen, the door open as it was warm weather in the school summer holidays. The children were out playing with their friends. Suddenly in dashed Tom, like a whirlwind as boys do, and up the stairs to his room. A few minutes later Edward and another boy appeared at the door.

'Where's Tom?' they asked.

'He's just gone upstairs, you can go up.'

Up they went, and then down they came.

'He's not up there.'

'He is! He's just dashed up there, go and look,' I said.

I was standing at the sink with a good view of the garden, and suddenly I saw Tom coming down the garden path.

He came in and I said, 'Your friends are upstairs looking for you, I thought you were already up there.' He looked at me in that way kids have, like they're thinking 'Yeah, OK Mum, whatever,' and up he went.

Well, *something* went up the stairs in a great hurry.

Carl worked in London at that time, and would sometimes meet a neighbour on the train. They would often stand outside the house chatting for a few minutes.

On one of these occasions he came in and said, 'Mandy's at her window.'

Both children were in bed as he didn't arrive home before 7.30 p.m.

'She can't be, I've been up there and she's fast asleep,' I said.

I was always lucky with my children. They went to sleep quite quickly and once they dropped off, it was very difficult to wake them up.

'She was there, she waved,' said Carl.

I went up and there she was, my little six-year-old, fast asleep.

The next day we asked her and she said no, she hadn't seen Dad from the window, but I knew she hadn't anyway.

A little child waving from the window. It was dark and Mandy's light wasn't on, so it wouldn't have been clear.

Obviously, you would assume it was Mandy.

Some three years later our family and some friends were sitting in the living room, the fire burning in the inglenook, when there was a sound of quick running footsteps across the long landing above.

'Sounds like there's a child up there,' said one of our visitors.

We all heard it, and all the children in the house heard it too, as they were all sitting with us.

I always felt extremely comfortable in this house, and we all loved it very much. I would sometimes spend nights there alone and always felt very happy and at peace. Also I learned a lot. Since I first arrived at the house calling Annie 'a mad woman', my mind had been opened up to new experiences and a new dimension of life.

Living in various houses in the future years, I never experienced anything as I did at that Hertfordshire house.

I eventually went to the spiritualist church with Deidre, my next-door neighbour on the other side to Annie. 'I've just started going, why don't you come? It's all fascinating,' she said.

I was a bit disappointed at first when we started singing Victorian hymns, the same as the church I had rejected from childhood. Then suddenly it was announced there was a visiting medium. Out of almost one hundred people, she picked me out. 'There is a fire all around you,' she said, 'but don't worry, it's a protective fire. I have two people in spirit who are looking after you and I can smell roses.' That was it. Aren't they supposed to give names? Usually there was something, like 'I'm getting a John or a Jim.' There were no names.

Very soon after this my mother and father visited. This was very rare as they now lived many miles away. I told them about the medium and I surprised myself as I would not normally have bothered to tell them, not expecting them to be sympathetic to this sort of thing, my mother being ensconced in the Church of England and my father being a pragmatist, with his practical and matter-of-fact way of approaching everything. I had another surprise, they responded! 'My mother loved roses,' said my father. 'Both grandmothers did,' said my mother. 'It must be Grandma and Nan then!' I said. I had been very close to both. They agreed. So I had got the final part from my parents, normally a most unlikely source.

When I first met Carl he was a calm, quiet person, but he proved not to be good in stressful situations. Carl was not good at coping with family life and would get impatient, eventually becoming abusive. I realised I had married too quickly, longing to leave the stifling home environment. I felt if I had given it more time and not rushed into marriage and babies, I would have seen he wasn't really cut out for family life. He would become irritable and I would be on the receiving end of harsh words. I had Nanna and Grandma, though.

Nanna would tell me stories about the early years of her

marriage, and how she and sister Rene heard about the first Marie Stopes clinic opening in London. It was the first opportunity for women's contraception, and they had never heard of anything like it before. She said she and Rene went in secret as it was quite daring, and you could only be seen by the clinic if you were married. She was issued with 'the cap' and said it served her well all her married life. There had been eight children in her family, and eleven in her husband's family. Nanna and Rene had two children each.

I would often take my children to Sudbury and stay with Grandma for a while, to get away and give us a break.

My father meanwhile had now taken a promotion and moved to Scotland with my mother, leaving the net curtains and stained glass windows behind, my mother mourning life in the 'posh' avenue. I didn't see my parents much after that. It was a very long way to travel, and we only had an 'old banger' for a car.

Then suddenly, they went even further away as another job came up in Northern Ireland. It was the time of the Troubles with the IRA and the work was in Belfast for the government. They were trawling for volunteers for Belfast unsuccessfully as the IRA were active and it wasn't an attractive proposition, even with promotion. 'You know, it's a chance to get back to London,' said Dad's boss. He knew my mother was desperately unhappy up there in Scotland and wanted more than anything to return to the net curtains. Dad reported back and Mum jumped at it. 'Of course you have to take it!' So he did, but they never returned to London. There never was such a clause. Was it made up to get rid of him? We reckoned so years later, and took it as evidence of the Asperger's again. 'Goodness knows what it must have been like to have to work with him,' remarked my brother on one occasion after yet another difficult exchange.

When my father went to work in Belfast, there was a job for my mother too, and it was at this time that I finally realised my mother should have been a career woman and was probably not truly happy bringing up a family. I think my mother was frustrated and unfulfilled as she had a very mathematical mind, brilliant for helping me with maths homework (I was hopeless at it) but that wasn't enough to fulfill her. Always having longed to go to university and work in a bank or similar, she had to content herself with being a housewife bringing up two children and I knew it wasn't enough. This means there was stress for her, and the trouble with stress is it affects people in so many different ways, and her way was retreating into herself. There must have been millions of women in the same position, and thank goodness things have changed now, with more opportunities than when I was young.

'I can't understand why your mother wants to move right over there!' said my grandmother on one of my regular visits to Sudbury in the old banger, me and the two little ones sharing a room for a night's stopover. 'She's missing all their dear little ways,' she would say, looking at my two toddlers. My mother had thrown herself into the work in Ireland and also the social life, which was constant, as it can be in the case of the Englishman abroad. She would write to me regularly, news about the latest dinner party, how they were both learning to drive, and the latest play or concert they had attended.

My mother would try to persuade me to come and visit on a free flight, one of their perks. I wouldn't, not with my little ones. 'Mrs So and So's daughter comes over all the time,' she would say. The denial and attitude to reality that she showed towards my father's behaviour now seemed to extend towards the situation in Northern Ireland.

Suddenly news came that my mother's boss had a bomb against his house. My father was called in the night and had to rush to the house, clothes over pyjamas, and help the family evacuate before the army bomb disposal started work. The bomb exploded and the house was badly damaged, luckily after the family had left. Another time my mother had taken a bus into Belfast city centre to collect a file from another office. 'I'd told her I didn't think it was a good idea,' said my father years later. As the bus approached the city centre, they blew up the bus station. It was a lucky escape. She was shaken by the experience and it strengthened my resolve not to go. I stood firm and never went there.

Sadly, Grandma was suddenly very ill and my mother flew over from Ireland on special leave to look after her at home in Sudbury, bringing her out of hospital as there was no more they could do for her; she needed nursing. My Aunty Lizzie, who had been a nurse, would come and stay too, and they took it in turns over the following few months to make Grandma as comfortable as possible. I went to Sudbury for the last time to see Grandma. She was still sweet and loving just like she always was. The doctor would come and drain off fluid from her lungs and each time she survived for a little longer. Finally, she died. There was just Uncle Harry left in Sudbury now. He would find himself a flat there, not wishing to be alone in the family house where they had lived for over forty-five years.

I was continuing with my work, now on a helpline for families in crisis. I did courses to understand abuse, particularly domestic abuse, and learned that domestic violence wasn't as I thought just physical, but meant also verbal, emotional and sexual abuse. I started to question my own life.

As time went on, Carl was not displaying the happiness he should have felt. He was still not good with the children and was still impatient and sometimes abusive towards me, and what was worse, to Tom. My other neighbour remarked on it to me; she had heard things through the wall. Eventually I decided we could not go on and went to a solicitor to file for divorce. I sometimes think that if couples' counselling had been available in those days we might have resolved things. There was nothing, however – I had never heard of such things, even though I worked on the helpline. I heard about people divorcing, but not getting professional help with their relationship. I couldn't get Carl to talk about it; he just got nasty.

I cried in the solicitor's office at every appointment, recounting my relationship with Carl as she prepared the papers. I suppose it was a kind of substitute for a counsellor; she did listen and was supportive and kind.

I remembered many years earlier going with Carl to see his mum and dad as we often did. I liked Carl's mum and dad a lot, they were very sociable and welcoming. I felt I had bonded with them, not having that easy relationship or the physical nearness with my own parents. This one time, we got to the front door and knocked as usual, and then realised we could hear shouting and crying. Finally his mother came to the door: 'Go away! You can't come in!' she screamed, tears streaming down her face. Carl turned away and I followed him down the path. 'What's going on?' 'Oh, they're often like that, we won't get like that,' he said. 'We certainly won't,' I said, still reeling. I was shocked. I had never experienced anything like this. My family were the opposite, seeming to express no emotion at all, so it was like a double shock. I realised later that the calm and quiet person, the Carl I had first met, was a person who did not express himself. No wonder he didn't trust himself to express anything, he didn't want to get like them. But all the feeling came out eventually, in his behaviour towards us. That was what his stress was all about, I decided, keeping things under wraps for so many years.

The divorce went through and Carl moved out to a flat at the end of the road. I had a lot of fallout to deal with as far as Tom was concerned.

It was also around this time that Nanna died. We had talked on the phone every week since my first baby was born. I couldn't believe I could dial her number and she wouldn't answer. She had told me recently how she was visiting 'old people', and how we had laughed at this as some of them were the same age or younger than her. She had been the only person to visit her mother-in-law, who had been horrible to her and virtually everyone else, and finally in her nineties ended up always alone as no one wanted to see her. Nanna had felt sorry for her, and was the only person who went there. This was typical of my lovely Nanna. When I went to the house on the day of her funeral, I couldn't believe she wasn't there.

To make ends meet I started to take in lodgers, students who were there for term time, leaving the house free for me and the children in holiday times. I started to socialise more and neighbours would invite me down to the pub in the evenings. The pub was only a couple of doors away and once the children were in bed and asleep and the students were there, I would go and have a chat for an hour or so. This is when I met Joe; he was always in the pub, and sometimes would call in for a chat on his way there, as I was almost next door. I was in love again and he was the reason why I finally moved to the country and also near to the sea, somewhere I had only dreamed of before.

Norfolk

I had always wanted to move further away from London, to live in the country or even better, near to the sea. When Joe suggested a new life in Norfolk, I jumped at the chance. He was a builder and had an idea to make a living. We would buy up cottages, which he would renovate, me helping as much as I could, and then sell them for a profit. He had the expertise and I had the money from the divorce. There was also our baby to look after, little Daisy, born eighteen months after our first pub meeting.

Sometimes it can be so difficult being a parent. Tom didn't want to come to Norfolk. It was understandable as he was now thirteen, that age when friends can become very important. After many arguments: 'I'd rather live with Dad,' he said. It had been very different now that Carl was living outside of the family. He was a lot better at relating to the children, and there wouldn't be that much pressure for him with only Tom, who was also older now. 'OK,' I said, 'you can stay with your Dad if you want to.' It was a big mistake. Within two years he was skipping school, and worse. I only found out about it a long time later when he talked to me about those years, explaining why he had ended up dropping out. If only we could go back and do things all over again. Talking on the phone from many miles away is not the same as being involved in the day-to-day detail of a child's life. What was I to do? I had thought taking a resentful teenager miles away from where they want to be was the worst option. If I didn't go, then the new life which I felt was so promising for us all couldn't happen and then Mandy would have been disappointed too. I still look back on this time and imagine the different scenarios that could have been. I can still feel the guilt from leaving him behind. Maybe reading this will help someone else to do things differently.

We left Hertfordshire for Norfolk with my divorce settlement and a car full, feeling and looking like the Beverly Hillbillies: a drugged dog (to prevent car sickness) a cat with a box of kittens (no experience of travelling with animals so the box placed in the back of the open estate), a baby (Daisy was three months old), and stacks of luggage including kitchen appliances packed at the last minute, which the friends who I had sold the house to decided they didn't want after all. It was very hot but we kept the windows closed, afraid a cat might jump out, or the dog Mandy was holding would jump out, or the baby I was holding would jump out… We arrived in the Norfolk village at our detached cottage 'in need of renovation'. Full of spiders and webs (a very elderly man having moved out some time ago, to go into care), we left it to Joe to find the hoover and make it acceptable for us to go inside. Luckily it was August, so we sat in the garden.

Norfolk was marvellous. It's a psychological fact that you need to be deprived of something to fully enjoy it and be very happy. After years of living in towns and London suburbs, the traffic-free and silent country lane, the garden full of wild flowers, and the smell of clean air, gave a wonderful feeling of being on holiday, and we were living there!

Joe renovated the cottage and I helped where I could, climbing the ladder to paint the new pebbledash pink. After a few months, the house was done and we named it Saddlers Cottage, as we found out it had something to do with horses. We sold it for almost twice what I had paid for it.

However, this idyll is not what it seems. I had met Joe in the pub and it turned out that he still needed to go to the pub, a lot, and the new start in life with our baby that he had so positively promised was not as positive as it should have been. Joe was a drinker, and that meant money, which was my money. At first, life was an adventure, working on the house in the week, and I enjoyed tending the garden and the very long piece of land attached to the house, full of home-grown vegetables and fruit. At weekends we all piled into the old car and headed for the coast or to explore other parts of Norfolk. Why shouldn't Joe go down the pub after a hard day's work?

All seemed normal, but soon the newer, more reliable car that I had bought was clocking up the miles of the pub rounds, and the bank balance was clocking up the beer money, plus the petrol, plus the boxes of wine. He was reverting back to his previous behaviour and it had to stop. The ultimatum was put in place, either he got some help, or he had to leave. He was not going to be allowed to destroy the family with debt or worse. But he wasn't strong enough; the drink won. I learned a lot about alcoholism and addictions at that time. I experienced first hand that addictions cannot be cured, however much you think you can help, unless the addict wants to be cured, and the addiction will always come first. Our relationship became non-existent, and anyway he already had a relationship – with drink. Drinking affected our sex life too; or rather it meant there was no sex life at all.

Eventually, after a few more months, with Joe hoping I might change my mind and turn a blind eye, he moved out, leaving me sighing with relief as I had been very worried about the bills and the future. I had never been in debt and was not willing to start, especially with two daughters to bring up. It was sad and rather tragic, as Joe had created and built a super place to live. He had so much talent but wasted it away.

It was after this second break-up that I thought of my grand-mother Ellen again, who had been so good to me and the children, and much loved. Grandma told me how she had realised a year after marrying my granddad George that she had made a mistake but had made her life in her four children. 'When he died it was a happy release,' she had said. My granddad had died nearly fifty years after they married, and it made me think of those times with no possibility of divorce and how miserable some people had to stay. I realised that in marrying Carl I had done something very similar to her, and had also rushed into a relationship with Joe at a vulnerable time, having not long been divorced and struggling with Tom, and the deaths of my dear grandmothers.

When I had first heard Grandma's story I would think to myself, now we have a choice to stay or go and those people who stay in abusive relationships may not feel the same if they knew they could never leave. Eventually though, I learned through my helpline training that it's not as simple as that, and how the pulls of the abusive relationship can be very strong with great ambivalence; it's a very complex matter. I learned to understand how the women became bonded to their partners, the same as in a healthy relationship, and when the violence happened, how they didn't feel it in the way that they would if it had been a stranger. Usually it was familiar anyway from childhood, as most of them came from abusive families where they had either been on the receiving end, witnessed it or heard it. It often has to get very bad before they start to feel it as a danger. I also learned it can be the same reasons for men abused by women or gay partners, but they often have nowhere to go, as domestic violence refuges are for women. I learned that somewhere in the world, every three days, a woman is killed by her partner.

I never knew the extent of my grandma's unhappiness. As a child staying with her, which I did regularly from the age of two, I would share a bed with my grandmother and would be woken early by the sound of a broom against the skirting board downstairs. Granddad would be sweeping, having got up early to do a few chores, and cook his own breakfast before going to work. Grandma would explain how this breakfast cooking was a 'fine art', putting all the eggs, bacon, bread and tomatoes in the frying pan on a very low gas ring, and 'by the time he's chored and shaved it will be cooked perfect,' she would say. Two cups of tea would appear for us, still in bed, mine very milky as I liked it then. This was kind and helpful of Granddad to Grandma, as it was a regular routine every morning. However I also remember he would return from work, have his tea, and then be seen lacing up his boots for his nightly visit to the pub, where he would stay; I never experienced him to be home in the evenings for the whole of the time I knew him. I never saw or heard him return from the pub, even in later years, so it must have been very late. My mother told me he never did that when they were children, but it was something that started when he returned from World War Two. I never saw Grandma and Granddad have a proper conversation or heard them laugh together. As a child I never thought anything of this, or of Granddad being out every night. It was what Granddad did. He died leaving debts. 'It was as if he gave up and nothing mattered anymore,' said my mother at the funeral. 'It was the drink that killed him,' some were saying. A general lack of motivation had caused the business to deteriorate, doing work for people and not charging enough, doing work for people he knew, and he knew a lot of people, and not charging them anything, but no one knew what was happening as he never spoke to anyone about it. Finally, Uncle Will going over the business accounts after the funeral was shocked at what he found. With his business past, he should have died maybe not a rich man, but certainly a man who was well off. For Grandma however, it was also 'a happy release'. She then told me how around fifteen years earlier, he had an affair with a policeman's wife. I was very surprised and a little shocked at this as I had no idea, but then typically the family would have kept it quiet with their ways, after all it would have been easier for them to deal with if they didn't actually talk about it. Apparently, Granddad had hit the policeman, luckily when he was off duty. I don't know why he did or any more of the story, except that it was on the Anglia news on the TV and was a nightmare for the 'keeping up appearances' family members. Grandma told me she then decided to leave him, but her two daughters, my mother and Aunty Lizzie, persuaded her not to. I remember thinking how unfair and selfish of them it was, and realising that Grandma was unable to stand up to them and do what she felt was best for her happiness.

It was after Joe moved out that I started with my work again. I was waiting with Daisy, aged three, to go into the weekly play-group, when I saw a flyer on the notice board, asking for people to be home visitors to families in crisis. A training was offered, and I knew I had to pursue it.

I worked with Home Start for nearly ten years as a volunteer home visitor. Visiting people in Norfolk was lovely, driving through the quiet countryside and the pretty villages, and I also got lots of interesting training. I managed to get some paid work in a women's refuge after my experience on the helplines and the domestic violence training. One of the most tragic examples of a negative family comes from this time.

When I first entered the refuge I was given a book to read: *Power and Control* by Sandra Horley, and it opened my eyes even further to the many things that constituted abuse. As well as emotional support, it was our job to try and help the women to feel the realities of the danger they were putting themselves in, so they wouldn't want to go back. This was especially important if they had children, which a lot of them did. If they did choose to go back, Social Services would get involved and sometimes the children would be taken away, as the mother was unable to protect them. Sometimes we had to watch as they went back to the abusive relationship, the pulls were too strong for them, but we were trained to recognise that they went back with things they hadn't had before; new knowledge and experience, awareness and information, and very often they eventually left again – for good this time.

Pattie had seven children – which can be more common in Norfolk than elsewhere I have lived – but she came into the refuge alone. The children had already been taken into care. She had been discovered sleeping on the floor, night after night, surrounded by the children, in a bid to protect them from the violent father. She couldn't, of course. After so many years trying to survive, the stress had caused her to have a mental breakdown and she was unable to care for the children. They were fostered out to various homes and she entered the mental health unit. She eventually arrived with us in recovery with depression, boxes of pills, and a suitcase. Many women that came into the refuge would suddenly relax and then realise how exhausted they were, often sleeping for hours on end, after years of living on their adrenalin. Pattie was one of the more extreme cases. At first she would sit on the floor in the corner of whichever room she happened to be in, the lounge, kitchen or the office, and continuously rock backwards and forwards in silence. Eventually though we managed to start some little conversations. I encouraged her to talk about anything she wanted. It transpired it wasn't just the life with her husband from which she carried all the problems; as a child she had suffered extreme neglect and abuse from both her parents. I marvelled at how someone suffering so much cruelty had survived to be one of the most gentle and caring people I had ever met. Her energy started to return and she started cleaning everywhere. The bathrooms were spotless, the large kitchen with the seven cookers, one for each family, was tidy and clear for the first time. She needed something to do. She missed her children dreadfully. She would speak to them on the phone, but sometimes they got upset and she couldn't do it. I encouraged her to write her thoughts down as it helped clear her mind. One day she came into the office to show me what she'd written, apologising in the same breath, 'I can't write'. As I read her large, round script without any gaps or punctuation, I started to see a poem there and wrote it all out for her again, but in a different way.

> My children are my life my hope my world
> You see I don't know a lot
> But the love I have got
> I thought was a lot
> I hope one day
> I can look back and say
> These thoughts
> Thoughts I have today

Have all gone away

Sometimes I cry a lot in one day
The truth is:
I don't think it will ever go away
My children
My life
My future

My happiness
My past
Gone

My love:
My seven little babies
My darling little people
Who one day will care for each other I hope

Life is short
Life is long
Hold it tight
Love it right
Because one day it will all be gone
Mine has gone

Who reads: make sure you hold on to yours
Take care
A message from someone who loves

I encouraged her to write more, and fed back to her the sensitive way she could write. Her confidence and self-esteem increased. She lived in hope that she might live with at least some or even one of her children again. They said it seemed unlikely. She wasn't even capable of living on her own yet and looking after herself. Eventually after a couple of years she was rehoused in her own flat. She still had support workers to visit. I never did find out if she lived with her children again. I couldn't help thinking of my family stories, and how it could have been very different if she had a wider circle of family – brothers and sisters maybe, or uncles and aunts who lived near, or lived with her – just how a lot of my family had been all those years ago. Sadly not everyone is so lucky.

Interesting Times

I was sent on a training session about communication and it changed some of my life, and also the lives of some of the people I was working with. We were told that we are always in one of three modes of communication: 'adult', 'parent' or 'child'. 'At the moment,' said the trainer, 'we are doing adult, but very often when we have arguments we can go into "child", calling each other names, sulking, slamming doors for example.' Apparently the way to do it was for both people to be in adult mode for it to work, listening to each other and discussing. If one person won't do this, we have to recognise that if they refuse to listen to us then we have to stop repeating ourselves, as the energy goes nowhere and we end up depleted, the situation unresolved. I liked the description of two adults arguing like children in the playground, name calling and shouting, and just like in the playground it needs an adult to come in and sort it out, meaning one of the people arguing has to go into adult mode, or ideally both people. We all had to think of some time in our lives when we were having some kind of similar unhealthy argument and then do what the trainer called a 'script rewrite'. It meant seeing the memory as a little scene from a play or film, and then give ourselves a different part to play, a different script. I immediately thought of my life with Carl where arguments were futile and if I tried to put my point of view, he could start to get abusive. I was told by the trainer I would have needed to go into parent mode with Carl as he was out of control, as well as being in child mode. This meant being very firm, sticking to the subject of the argument and not being drawn into defending myself or going down other paths into other subjects, also telling Carl what he was doing, and if all else failed, to withdraw, but to tell him I was withdrawing and why. This all had to be done in a very firm way like I really meant it, just as a very firm but kind, calm parent would do, and not in a tearful way for example, as that apparently would just be child again. As I thought about this I realised that for a very long time I had communicated with Carl the very same way my family had approached anything negative or 'bad'; I had said nothing. I just let him carry on, let him do it, and I hadn't even realised. Eventually when I had started to stick up for myself, he had just got worse, but then all I was doing was defending myself and that, according to the trainer, doesn't work either, as that was child too. I went forward in a new way after that training. I felt more confident, like I had found a part of myself that was now going to be in control and not allow any rubbish from anyone. Life would have been very different if I could have been like this with Carl, I thought, but then I may not have tolerated him in the first place. This way of communication proved hugely successful as I worked with people who had low self-esteem or felt bullied by someone. We would look at how we could go into parent mode, or maybe just adult mode depending on the situation, and they would eventually decide what they actually wanted to say. Their partners would benefit too when they heard about the two children in the playground thing, and very often during an argument, one might say 'We're doing it again! Let's go back into adult!'

Sticking to the subject we are arguing about, bringing it back if it's gone on to something else, thinking 'discussion' instead of argument, all these tools changed a lot of lives, including my own.

As I went on with more training and studying, I realised that my brother may have something in common with my Uncle Harry. Whereas I had left home as soon as possible, and didn't see my parents any more than I had to these days, Andy had never married or lived with any girlfriend, and in his thirties was still holidaying with our mum and dad, not really enjoying it as there were always moans about it to me when he came home. My mother, Mary, just like her mother, Ellen, seemed to have put her close emotional relationship in her son, as she couldn't have one properly with my dad because of the Asperger's. Unlike Uncle Harry, Andy was able to actually leave home, eventually buying his own place, being of a different personality to Harry – stronger. I remember Andy many years later when we were reminiscing saying, 'I'd just got it all together in London, made quite a few friends and had plans to house-share when Mum told me she wanted me to live in that flat they bought in Surrey.' And he did, leaving his new-found social life behind and doing what his mother wanted. He luckily managed to resist her plea to go up to Scotland where she felt so lonely, at a time when he was studying at the Royal College for his music degree. Thank goodness, as that would have halted any future career in music. As I studied, and read more and more, I decided years later his subsequent long affair of several years with a married woman was his way of staying 'faithful' to his mother. To satisfy the two pulls: to do what mother wants and to do what he naturally needed to do.

What happened to our mother? She developed several complaints where tests found nothing wrong, and the complaints were diagnosed as psychological. She lost her sense of taste and saw many specialists for this one, but nothing could be found. She suffered from IBS and various other stomach problems; again nothing could be found. The loss of taste she had for five years before she told me.

More Paranormal

I am in my sociology class, working towards my social care certificate, and sitting next to me is Cindy, a bright, happy young woman. We had 'clicked' straight away and would often have long conversations about the work and our lives.

On this particular day, Cindy suddenly turned to me and said, 'I can see Victorian children playing.' My reaction was one of great interest, as I knew what she meant straight away, being already familiar with experiences like this.

'I've always seen them, ever since I was a little girl. I thought everyone could see them but I soon realised no one else could, so I stopped talking about it. I don't see them all the time – they come and go, I can see them now.' It was part of her life which she accepted as normal. It hadn't caused her any problems. Our friendship continued through the two years we were studying at the college. Cindy went on like me to get a job as a support worker.

Almost five years later, I ran into her in Tesco – literally almost colliding with our trolleys. She was still happy, living with her husband and now a baby too. We never spoke of her Victorian children after that one time. For Cindy it was no big deal, they'd always been there, part of normal life.

Since my experiences in the Hertfordshire house, I was always comfortable and very curious when people told me these kinds of stories.

Back in my home a new carpet had been long overdue, and here was the carpet layer to fit it, a pleasant and friendly man. After a bit of a chat, I left him in the cleared lounge and went upstairs to do some work.

Later I came down to offer a cuppa and after a few pleasantries he said, 'There's a lady by your door at the bottom of the stairs.'

This was interesting, as I hadn't experienced anything out of the ordinary in a house since moving from Hertfordshire.

'Really? Do you know who she is?'

'No, but I get this sometimes, always have done in fact, as far back as I can remember.'

He went on to say he thought it was fine to tell me as he assumed I would be familiar with these things; he'd noticed all the hanging wind chimes and candles around the house!

He said he would often see or hear things in people's houses where he was working. He didn't always tell them as he often felt they wouldn't be sympathetic or want to hear it. He gave an example of a young mum who left him in her house while she collected her child from school. After about half an hour had gone by, he could hear clattering noises of crockery in the kitchen and talking. He went through hoping for the offer of a cuppa, and found there was no one there. The house was empty and quiet. The young mum returned with the child about fifteen minutes later, confirming that there couldn't have been anyone else there, and he was able to joke it away.

He was quite comfortable with his experiences, telling me his grandmother had been the same and it was 'in the family'.

A neighbour of mine had a pacemaker fitted and there he was, sawing his wood for the fire as usual. 'Should you be doing that so soon?' I asked him. 'Oh, it's fine!' he said. 'The doc says I can be normal now.' Then he went on to say he'd had 'one of those experiences.'

During the operation he had a dream where he'd seen a white light and a tunnel. It had felt wonderful, so much love, and he had very strongly wanted to go up it. After the operation he told the surgeon about the dream. 'Well, we lost you for a few minutes!' said the surgeon. 'He seemed familiar with my story,' said my neighbour. 'He'd obviously heard it before.' My neighbour's heart had stopped during the op and luckily he was revived. 'I tell you what, I've got no fear of death now!' he said.

Hearing these stories meant that when I encountered the world of 'healing', I was quite comfortable with the sort of people I was to meet there.

Health and Healing

It's a big shock to be suddenly told you have cancer. A friend had said 'You should go and get that checked,' noticing a continuous bloodshot spot on my eye. But I didn't bother. Eventually the small bloodshot area became a bright red protruding spot, and then turned brown, starting to grow outwards and becoming very uncomfortable. I went to my lovely doctor who got me an appointment at Addenbrookes immediately. They recognised it straight away and got me an appointment at Barts in London for the following day. It was a very rare eye cancer.

I spent some time that evening alone, contemplating a tumbler of sherry, and thinking about death. I decided I could face death if it wasn't for my children. I felt they had no one else, especially Daisy. I had to live.

I was told only three surgeons dealt with this type of cancer: one in America, one in Australia, and one in London. People came from all over the world to this Barts Hospital department. While I was in the waiting room, I suddenly felt lucky. A lady spoke to me about a terrible decision she had to make. Her cancer was behind her eye, and her other eye was barely functional. She could have the cancer removed but it would leave her blind. If it wasn't removed she had about five years to live, she had been told. She was thinking five years of a good life with sight might be preferable to blindness for the rest of her life.

I met two men who each had a false eye. How marvellous modern medicine is – the replicas looked real and actually moved with the normal eyes. Of course, they couldn't see out of the false eyes. 'It's OK,' they said, 'we can still drive with one eye, though not at night.' I thought I would be able to handle that. It had suddenly occurred to me that my eye might have to be removed. When I saw the consultant he told me they could remove the brown spot from the white of the eye and replace with donor white. The eye needn't be removed and I had the chance of a long and happy life, he said. Now I felt extremely lucky. I checked in three days later, had the op, and felt very relieved. However, it wasn't over. 'Now you need a liver scan and a chest X-ray to see that it hasn't spread,' said the nurse. I was glad they hadn't told me that before. It may have been just too much to cope with. It turned out to be all clear, and I was discharged, coming out into the autumn air, marvelling at the brightness and the colours of the leaves, which I could still see. From the window of my ward I had seen a little church and had resolved that if I came out successfully, I would go into this church and give thanks. I was able to light a candle in there, and it changed my approach to churches. They didn't have to be boring and meaningless places. They could be whatever I wanted them to be.

It was Ian who looked after me then. I had recently married Ian because he wanted to get married. We were together four years and the marriage lasted for one year. Mandy had now left home for uni, a very bright future ahead of her. Daisy was eight and having been without a father for as long as she could remember, I thought it was a good idea. Ian gave her lots of attention, and he and I shared a love of walking. We walked the whole of the Offa's Dyke path together from South to North Wales, Ian carrying the tent and cooking stove, me bearing a lighter load.

A psychic at a party my friend persuaded me to go to ('She's ever so good, it's only £5!') had told me I was going to meet a man who would take me to lots of places. If only I had listened properly. Marriage wasn't mentioned.

The bit about lots of places was spot on. As well as Offa's Dyke, Ian and I walked all over Norfolk, Suffolk and Lincolnshire. Both Daisy and myself enjoyed trips with him to York and the Moors, Hadrian's Wall, the Welsh coast, The Jurassic Dorset coast, the Lleyn Peninsula, the Pembrokeshire coast, and the Mallorcan mountains. We went to jazz clubs, blues clubs, skiffle clubs and rock clubs.

The trouble started when we married. Ian became like a big brother to Daisy, and not a nice one. I now know that we never really know anyone until we live with them and marriage can cause changes in behaviour, but I didn't know this then.

Like Carl, Ian was unable to face his behaviour. Not in an aggressive way, but just through denial. As far as he was concerned it either never happened, wasn't quite like that, or was someone else's fault. Once I was well again, I left, removing Daisy from the unhealthy environment. It was easy to leave. Previous experience had made this a complete turn-off. There were going to be no more repetitions like Carl.

But first I had to get through my operation. When I returned from hospital after my eye operation, I wasn't allowed to read or watch TV for three weeks. Ian proved to be a natural housekeeper and nursemaid. He cooked all the meals, did the washing, saw Daisy to school, and brought me audio book tapes from the library. For those who believe that certain people are sent to us for a reason at certain times, this is surely a good example.

Eventually, the eye patch off and allowed to read again, I saw an advert in the local newspaper: 'Free Healing'. I wonder what that's all about, I thought. Well, it's worth trying anything, I'll go along.

She sat me in a hardback chair and asked me a bit of my history. I told her I'd had this recent operation. 'Just relax,' she said. I contemplated the wall in front of me. She stood behind me for a while and nothing happened. Suddenly I had the sensation she had left me, she wasn't there anymore. Feeling slightly annoyed I turned my head, only to see her hand very close to my face. She was standing behind me; both arms outstretched each side of my body. How peculiar, I definitely thought she'd gone. I settled down once more and she worked her hands slowly down my body, not touching me at all. Suddenly, I felt very hot and slightly dizzy. 'I think I'm going to faint,' I said. She stopped immediately and poured me a drink of water from the jug on the side. 'It's because it's so soon after your operation,' she said. 'Your energy field is quite low and now the energy is rushing in.' 'Energy field?' 'Yes, it's part of you, it's all around your body. Some people call it the aura.' I was amazed. She hadn't touched me at all but something was obviously happening. After a while I felt better and she started again. This time it was all right and I felt a lovely tickly feeling come over me. When she'd finished I thanked her, left a donation and resolved to return.

'Wow! There's certainly something in that,' I said to Ian. 'She never touched me.'

I went at least a dozen more times, each experience becoming more lovely and relaxing, until Jan (who ran the sessions) said to me, 'I'm starting a new course for people to become healers, you're welcome to come along.'

When I went into the healing training I met people who could 'see things'. We were taught how to develop our sensitivity, to feel, and sometimes for some, to actually 'see' the energy field or aura (which can now be measured electronically, so we know it exists and consists of various colours, we were told). I saw an energy field once. We did an exercise of relaxation and meditation and then one of us sat on a chair a few yards from the others, and we all concentrated. I saw a white light all around their body. Not fortunate enough to have the gift of 'second sight' as it can be called, I wasn't able to see the colours that one or two of the others saw. 'Everyone sees the same colours so you'll know what we're seeing exists,' they would say.

Anyone can heal, we were told; it's an ability we all have. The universal healing energy that surrounds us can be channeled through us and into another person; they then will take it in. This is usually done unconsciously so we need not worry where it's going. It will be used where needed. The person doing the healing needs to have good intent, and not have anger or other negative feelings, as this can interfere with the good intent. Jan realised I was ready for the training although she hadn't known that I had gone through some sessions of personal therapy as part of my training where I had managed to work with and rid myself of angry feelings I had felt in the past towards both my mother and my father. I had also managed to explore the issues of my mother's detachment, as well as some of my experiences with my partners.

I befriended Nora in the training group and we would meet up and practice our healing. These times were lovely, full of relaxation and feelings of being cared for. Nora wasn't a 'seer' but sometimes she could sense things. 'When I'm on your left side, the word "child" keeps coming into my head,' she said at one session. We had a little discussion about this and wondered if it was to do with the 'inner child'.

Bobby, a young man in the training group and a karate teacher, was a very sensitive 'seer'. He would enter the group saying, 'We have a lot of visitors tonight,' and he didn't mean 'people' in the usual sense. I couldn't see anything. On this particular evening, Bobby was just finishing my healing when he said to me, 'There's an angel by your left shoulder. It's very small, like a child with long fair hair.' Immediately, I remembered what Norah had said a few weeks earlier when standing on my left side, 'The word "child" keeps coming into my head.' And then Annie all those years ago, 'One of your guides is a child.' It was like it was saying to me, 'Now do you believe it? I am here!' I left the group that night with a lovely tickly feeling and quite humbled, but excited.

Such a high proportion of people with this second sight are involved in healing groups and healing therapies that 'seeing' seems to have a connection to love and caring, I thought. One night I was walking home from the group when I suddenly had an experience I had never had before. I felt I was still there, in the group with them all, and I had the most wonderful feeling of love and belonging. I thought that if everyone could experience this, no one would ever feel lonely.

How It Ended Up

Some years before, my mother had decided to write what she called her 'memoirs'. At that time, I had started looking at very old family photos and asking who they all were, and she said, 'I'll write my memoirs and then you'll have some history.' She wrote about her childhood and her experiences in the war, up until when she married my father, Frank. When I read it I was amazed, struck with some of the expressiveness of the writing. She had never in my whole life been able to talk to me like this. When I saw she had been frustrated in her ambition for uni and her love of maths, I felt for her, as I knew what it was like to have a pull for something that you feel is such a big part of yourself. I had been able to fulfil mine. I was starting to understand her better.

My relationship with my father gradually improved after my mother died. Having lived in denial to the end, she was suddenly given two months to live but she was dead within a week. Cancer had spread right through her body.

Dad and I started to talk on the phone regularly, something we had never done as it was always Mum who phoned me, and told me the news. This new relationship was going to be very 'real', I decided. No more ignoring and saying nothing when he engaged his defences of denial and needing to be right, his behaviour sometimes even bordering on abuse. It started with a lot of challenge, and when I went to visit, often ended with me shouting and sometimes leaving. Eventually however we came to a point where he had started to think about what he was doing, not that he would ever say so of course, but his behaviour started to change a little. I gradually got used to challenging him in a firm way, the frustration of many years gradually dissipating. He needed me now as there was no one left apart from my brother. If my mother had been alive it would have been far more difficult, if not impossible, to build a relationship in this way. He would have been able to hide behind her protection of denial and her expressions of horror. 'Don't talk to your father like that!' It wasn't allowed. I began to notice how much worse he became when under stress and realised how a family with little children would have been a big strain for him. I was now able to relate to him as I had an understanding of what was happening. As long as I didn't have any unrealistic expectations, this relationship could exist in a positive way. I remembered his stories of his own childhood and how he had never spoken of his sister Emily's tragic accident, and I had never asked him, somehow picking up that I mustn't. 'Do you remember when Aunty Emily went blind?' I said to him one day. He thought for quite a time, a frown on his face. Finally, 'When did we move to Surrey?' 'You were about eleven. Remember? You went to a new school?' More thinking and silence. Finally I said, 'Can you remember what it was like? When you got home from school that day?' 'I can't remember,' he replied. 'It must have been awful for everyone,' I said.

And then he said such a strange thing. 'In what way?'

He seemed to be completely out of touch with what I could mean, as he sat there frowning. In what way could it be awful to come home from school to find your sister is suddenly blind? To find the family in who knows what sort of state? It doesn't bear thinking about, but perhaps that's the clue. He had blocked it out, unable to cope with that memory full of other emotions in which he couldn't participate. But also I had heard about the Asperger memory; my support work had given me the knowledge that people with Asperger's very often don't remember things like other people do. 'Numbers – no problem!' said one very nice man I worked with for a while. 'But situations – they seem to slip away very easily.' 'Our minds and memories work differently,' said another.

Another event I talked to Dad about was when he was diagnosed with a tumour on his thigh. He had been fourteen and had an operation to remove it. The scar on his leg was very long and prominent, with what looked like the marks of some very crude stitching.

Me: 'What do you remember about your tumour op? Did it stop you playing football for a while?' (He loved his sports.)

Dad: 'I don't remember. (Long thinking.) I was in St Thomas' hospital in London for three weeks. It was the summer months, so it wouldn't have interfered with football.'

Me: 'Do you remember what it was like in hospital?'

Dad: 'It was my first experience with dying. The elderly man next to me died.'

Me: 'What was that like?'

Dad: (Long thinking.) 'I don't remember.'

Me: 'Do you remember coming home and not being able to walk too well?'

Dad: (Long thinking.) 'I don't remember.'

Anyone reading this conversation may not guess that the person answering the questions is a person who loves to talk; a person who always likes to be an instigator of communication. The answers indicate struggling. Also they are very factual. Trying to get any information about the way he felt, getting him to express his emotions, was impossible.

At ninety-four, he is now in care. As well as his completely self-centred moments of communication, an expression of concern for me can suddenly surface, and affection, which in the distant past had caused me frustration and puzzlement that the two could go hand-in-hand, but now I understood. Carers have gradually got to know him and come to expect his ways and deal with them firmly. When other people say to me, 'What a lovely man, your father!' I smile at them, thinking, 'Yes, but if you *really* knew him... '

Eventually Daisy left home for uni as Mandy had done. When Daisy left for uni, I found myself living alone for the very first time in my life, and I realised I loved it. I loved to be able to get up very early if I wanted to without disturbing anyone and experience that magical time when the light is breaking, the stillness and the peace. I loved to be able to be up in the night and be working and then sleep until midday. I loved to be able to fill the house with beautiful classical music, to be able to eat what I want, when I want, to have who I want in the house when I want, to be able to go away for days on end whenever I want, to be able to do all of these without causing disturbance for anyone else. The list could go on. All the years of living in a family, with a man, with children, I was now free to experience a relationship with myself, seeing my friends and enjoying my interests. I realise now, as long as my children are happy, I am happy. We are all close. I can't go back and change anything in the past, but I can build on the future. The bond with them is strong. This was becoming another of the happiest times of my life. I paid a visit to the friends I had kept in touch with in Hertfordshire including Annie, who read the cards for me. She read, 'The cycle of sorrow and pain has finally come to an end. Be at peace with your healing. You have walked the path of true courage, now is the time to go out into the world and live the life you were born to live.' We never met again, as she died soon after.

Under The Hood Part 4

The Children

'We are psychologically healthy when our quest for knowledge is uninhibited.'

Sigmund Freud.

'Don't speak.' 'Don't feel.' 'Don't be yourself.' 'Don't tell people your problems.' 'Don't listen to yourself, listen to what I want.'

These are some of the 'childhood messages' we can see in the stories; they are common, and they come from the way the adults relate to the children.

Childhood messages can cause problems in adulthood; for example low self-esteem, suppression or anxiety. Positive messages cause healthy emotional growth.

How we view ourselves will have a big impact on who we attract into our lives. Where does this view come from? It comes from the way the adults relate to us and what they tell us. For example, not reacting or engaging when a child speaks can give the message, 'I am not worth listening to.'

Jilly says she and her brother blamed themselves for not being able to relate to their father. No one gave them any indication of the truth, that it was Frank's problem. We are told he was allowed to carry on with his behaviour without anyone commenting. This will give the children the message that Dad is OK, that this is normal. So if Dad is OK it must mean I am not, it must be me.

Jilly's mother Mary is not relating easily to her, but has invested her emotional relationship in Jilly's brother Andy. What message does this give Jilly?

When we hear Jilly say 'to finally marvel at the outside world with so many people in it who wanted to relate and listen to what I had to say, and more importantly respond to it as well,' we hear relief, a feeling of freedom at last, an excitement that the whole world is not the same as her parents' world.

Children need the adults to be OK for their own little world to be secure, so this also means they can easily blame themselves for an adult's behaviour.

Carrying anger towards her mother and father, Jilly manages to discharge childhood feelings in therapy as an adult. She also has 'marvellous friends' in her life, so there would have been some discharge here as she says she can be herself with them.

Anger towards parents by the child is normal if natural needs are not being met. It can be common in abusive situations for the child to be angry with the parent who is not the abusive one. One of the reasons for this is because of their thinking 'Why don't they do something about it?' Very often, the child is angry with both parents. Using anger tools (see the chapter 'Anger') to express feelings, then understanding her parents' behaviour, Jilly would be able to think differently about her childhood situation, to understand it, and herself. This would raise self-esteem, rid her of damaging anger, and any other feelings that surface from the past.

When Jilly says she has to 'deal with the fallout' with Tom, after the divorce, we are seeing a case of a child's reactive behaviour. After the experience of his father's abusive behaviour towards his mother and himself, Tom would have been left with a lot of confusing feelings. Children invariably display these feelings where they feel safe. We often hear how children returning from a difficult visit to an estranged parent, or after a stressful day at school, will 'behave badly' when they return, and it is a parent who gets the reactive behaviour. Once Carl has left the family unit it will be safe and calm, perfect for Tom to start expressing his feelings. Children's minds are not mature enough to talk about their feelings like adults can, so they can express their feelings in their behaviour.

Mary's behaviour as a child, being difficult with the first child carer when her mother Ellen was giving birth, and a few years later her behaviour with the second child carer and her sixteen-year-old daughter, is typical reactive behaviour in a child unable to verbally express how she feels. 'I would call them names, out of earshot I hope now! I remember being very difficult and uncooperative.' Although she was much older in the second incident, it would have triggered all the feelings from the first incident, and carrying this early baggage could have caused quite forceful behaviour.

Very often if you ask a child how he or she feels, they won't know. When we work with children we use a picture sheet of various cartoon faces in expressions of sadness, happiness, anger and so on. The child can then pick the face he or she thinks best applies to them. This is also a good way to help children generally to get used to connecting with their feelings.

Same household, same upbringing; how come children can turn out so differently? One of the answers is personality. Caring trait, selfish trait, a leaning to introvert or extrovert, strengths and weaknesses, maturity, immaturity, all will have a bearing on the result. Another reason is that even in the same household, upbringing experiences can be different. Jilly's experience will be very different from her brother Andy, as their mother is relating to them in a different way, and so is their father. Experiences with sibling relationships, and position of birth in the family, relationships with extended family and family friends, will all have a bearing.

Jilly

The first little story from Jilly tells us two things: that Jilly is a sensitive child, sensitive to other people and how they are feeling and that Jilly's mother Mary may be depressed, or at least is certainly

117

not happy. It is a poignant scene with her mother bent over the sink and the pile of washing-up, Jilly desperately feeling she wanted to help, but longing to join the other children in the garden. Even at the young age of six, Jilly is displaying her natural ability to pick up the signals that someone is struggling or is not happy, an ability that is going to stand her in good stead, and one of the reasons why she became so drawn and attuned to her work supporting people. At six years old, the child part of her is of course strong, and she ends the scene by skipping out into the sunshine.

There are not many memories of her mother but there are many other early memories with her extended family. This tells me her relationship with her mother was not a close one.

From what we hear, Mary was frustrated at not being able to pursue a university career. She loved mathematics, thinking she would like to work in a bank, but that too was a closed door because of the attitudes of that time. The outlet for this part of her is not being allowed expression. This alone can cause an unhappiness; a feeling of non-fulfillment. There may even have been part of her that just didn't want to be there with the children, but that part could also have carried guilt, making even more to shoulder. Today she would be able to use this strong part of her in part-time work or a successful career. She would have choices for a career alongside childcare. Jilly has inherited her father's humanitarian qualities with the pull for working to help people. She is using this part of herself, her natural ability, which brought her much fulfillment and contentment; something her mother was unable to do with her own natural ability.

Another possible reason for her mother's unhappiness is her relationship with her husband. Not just because of the Asperger's Syndrome, although that would over time present difficulties as there was a lack of awareness and understanding, but because of the resulting defence mechanisms Frank employed. It would be very difficult as time went by to converse when denial and always having to be right, to name but two of the issues, are continually employed by one partner.

Jilly's personality is very different from the rest of her family, as she feels the need to be genuine, to acknowledge the bad stuff, to talk about everything, to be expressive. Her mother tries to curb this, and has a fear of acknowledging the negative things along with the rest of the family. Things are 'swept under the carpet' as she shies away from any involvement to help the children in their communication with their father, and is afraid of what people think; a fear that causes denial and pretence. If Frank's family was able to have the knowledge we have today, Asperger's Syndrome could have been a very different story for him as his family was accepting and open with Archie's epilepsy, which they understood.

Jilly eventually manages to escape what she calls a 'stifling environment' and finds great fulfillment in her work. Studying and training over the years, as well as expressing her true self, she also comes to understand more about her family's behaviour.

The benefit for Jilly was her relationships with other people apart from her parents, primarily her grandmothers, who she tells us she was closer to than her mother. The grandmothers are able to relate to Jilly and she feels a lot of love for them.

Jilly also says she has 'marvellous friends'. Very often people with dysfunctional families or no families compensate with close positive relationships outside the family. Life can sometimes be much happier this way, as we can choose our friends but not our families. If Jilly had not had the benefit of extended family, or other adults to learn to relate to, she could have found herself with more problems as she grew up. She acknowledges the resulting trouble she experienced being in some group situations.

Because of her personality, wanting to change negative things and acknowledge reality, Jilly is well suited to her role of support worker and is able to engage in personal therapy to rid herself of her internal anger and frustration relating to her father and her mother. Jilly's anger towards her mother could indeed have been stronger than her anger with her father, as mentioned before: children will very often see the parent who is not behaving in an abusive or negative way towards them as the one at fault, because they did nothing to change things in the family environment. Jilly is able to relate to her father through their shared abilities at physical activities, while the relationship with her mother can seem almost non-existent; another reason why anger can be directed towards her mother.

Jilly is able to tell us about her mother's brothers and sister, and to sometimes explain their behaviour. 'The uncle who never spoke' is particularly quite tragic. Will, the same little boy full of curiosity who badgered his father to show him a dead body has been brought up by his father with no talking allowed, having to behave in a certain way, and with a male role model of a withdrawn parent unable to demonstrate emotion. The combination of a child's personality plus the adoption of certain behaviours (whether through fear or in an attempt to get closer to a parent by imitating them) can result in extremes.

It would seem Jilly's personality is similar to her father's, and Andy's personality has more in common with their mother. Andy bonds closer to his mother because of this and Jilly bonds closer to father, which brings distress. ('I remember crying myself to sleep, my mother stroking my face.') Jilly and her father enjoy their love of physical activity together, and Jilly is out in the world like he also was as a child; both have a humanitarian side, and a draw to help people. He is sociable and likes to talk, and she loves to talk, which is why she found relating to a withdrawn mother so hard. Andy is retreating at home in his mother's company, not having the need for looking outwards into the world, or sharing the need for physical activity. He is also his mother's prime emotional relationship, a replacement for her husband, which is unhealthy relating. Mary repeats her mother's behaviour of emotionally investing in her son. Andy's behaviour is different to Harry in that he does not stay with his mother throughout life, but he does stay emotionally invested, illustrated by the long relationship with the married woman at a young age.

When we read Mary's memoirs, it is a good example of writing for release. Unable to express herself easily and talk about negative things, she pours a lot of emotion into The Mother's Story. This can be a tool for clients who find it difficult to talk: discharging emotion through writing.

When Jilly reads the memoirs, she is struck by the fact her mother could never talk to her like she writes. By reading it, Jilly starts to connect with her mother, to understand and empathise, showing how sharing parts of ourselves with another can promote closer relating.

Jilly can relate to her father on a certain level but there are problems because of the ignorance and denial of the Asperger's.

Asperger's Syndrome

When Mary met Frank, his inability to connect in a close way would have been apparent but it would also have been familiar, as her father George was unable to connect in a close way. Familiar can mean comfortable and it would have been more difficult to spot in Frank. He is not remote like George; in fact he is entirely opposite. Sociable and communicative, seeking out social situations, the Asperger's would have been apparent, but would also have been easy to deny in the first flush of love and romance. As Jilly says of her father, people would first of all see him as 'a lovely man' but eventually, over time, people would get to know the other part of him, the part that has difficulty with expressing emotion and relating, with the resulting defence mechanisms. Mary can feel comfortable with it because of the familiarity, and not even feel it to start with, but eventually, later, she will feel the effects.

Asperger's Syndrome is on the autism spectrum, where social interaction and communication are difficult. It is called a 'spectrum disorder' as the symptoms can vary in strength from person to person. Men can have a tougher time than women, because of differences in male and female chromosomes: women generally have it easier, picking up signals of communication. A person with Asperger's Syndrome can find it hard to work out what other people are feeling or thinking. Picking up cues in conversation can be impossible, so it can be easy to talk over people, or maybe even suddenly start a completely unrelated conversation before the current one is over. As Jilly says they can appear rude without meaning to. Other types of personalities with Asperger's Syndrome may be discouraged from talking at all. Small talk and chat can be very difficult as the world for people with Asperger's Syndrome is a very logical one; they are very good at picking up facts and details and can have a lot of patience concentrating on lengthy tasks, but their conversation very often focuses on these interests, rather than the human or emotional aspect. A small incident but a good example is when Jilly at about three years old is covered in bandages from the scalding and her father remarks, 'She looks like a nun!' This statement is a very common reaction with Asperger's, as Jilly's father is logically stating what he is seeing and thinking, without feeling a connection to Jilly.

Imagination can be a troublesome area for a person with Asperger's Syndrome, as they are often unable to visualise something that doesn't exist in their reality. Social situations can become confusing, and depending on the personality, any social insensitivity could get worse as the person with Asperger's struggles to cope in a world they often feel they don't understand. Indifference to loved ones can be demonstrated.

Acknowledging and talking about these difficulties from an early age makes it far less stressful as the person doesn't feel they have to pretend everything is OK and subsequently build up negative defence strategies to survive. Unfortunately, Jilly's mother Mary continues the family's status quo of denial, and Frank continues his defence mechanisms: always having to be right or denying something negative was said by him, using projection to accuse the other person of the same or some other negative behaviour, which sometimes becomes abusive. Frustrating for any person trying to communicate in a normal way, it would have been devastating for a sensitive child like Jilly, trying to connect with her father. Both Jilly and her brother would have suffered greatly as children, struggling with no help from the other adults around them. It is not surprising that they would blame themselves for not being able to relate to their father. The lack of acknowledgement or help gave the children the message that Dad is OK, but they are not. It can be common for children to blame themselves for the adults' shortcomings, as they need their world to be secure, and if the adults are not OK, then their world does not feel secure. The result is that the child believes it must be they who are at fault.

Those with Asperger's Syndrome are commonly bright or of superior intelligence, and have great potential to be capable, talented and successful people, so Jilly's father was well able to have a place on the local council and a career in the Civil Service. It would only be when certain situations popped up that there would have been problems, as it seems there eventually were, both in the council and the everyday working environment.

Asperger's has been recognised as responding well to CBT, but as in all therapeutic situations the person in the therapy needs to be able to accept and take responsibility for what they are doing. Asperger's or no Asperger's, no therapy will work with the kind of personality weakness that cannot take responsibility for their own behaviour, or acknowledge it. This type of personality will build up their own defence mechanisms of denial, lying, distorting events, pretended memory loss, or saying nothing in response to another who is trying to resolve a problem situation. Did Frank have this personality? The evidence is there that he did. He continued through life in the same way, never acknowledging his behaviour. When Jilly starts to relate to her father in a different way, Frank starts to realise what he's doing, and starts to do things differently but as Jilly says, 'not that he would ever say so, of course,' which indicates the weakness in him. His family never acknowledged his behaviour and ignored it, allowing him to dominate conversations, giving him permission to continue in his weak way.

Working with Asperger's, communication techniques can be learned with a factual approach as the old ways are acknowledged and discarded, and intellectual awareness and an understanding of what is happening are gained.

If Jilly had a role model for how to deal with her father, the bonding between them could have been a lot stronger. If Frank had been able to relate in a genuine way and acknowledge his difficulties, then the bond would have been strengthened. Sharing of ourselves brings intimate relating. She would have been able to understand him better and not feel so isolated, adapting in the way that children can. Similar in personality with their loves of physical activity, sports, walking and swimming, Jilly and her father share these and this helps to bring them closer together. Activities can be a good bonding mechanism when emotional connection is lacking. It is not that the person with Asperger's Syndrome never feels emotion; it is the expression of that emotion that can be very difficult – if not impossible. It is in the relating to others that the main difficulties lie.

Family life is all about relationships and communication: relationships between partners, parents and children, brothers and sisters, and extended family members. Asperger's Syndrome is all about challenges in communication, misunderstandings of social cues, and lack of understanding emotionally. Every relationship in the family is affected.

Asperger's Syndrome was unheard of in the days of Frank's childhood; when autism itself was largely unknown. There have been subsequent studies that link Asperger's Syndrome with flu in pregnancy. In Frank's story, we hear how his Uncle Archie had fits and Frank was familiar with hearing, 'That's Archie, he's the epileptic.' Sadly, there was no label for Frank so he could not be understood as Archie was. The behaviour, ignored and denied by the family's fears, could not get any better, and had every chance of getting worse. Unfortunately, if we ignore something bad it often gets worse – and almost never disappears.

Jilly's Question

There could have been many questions from Jilly, but a lot she has managed to answer for herself as she becomes more aware with her

124

work and training. All her partners are displaying a weakness of personality in being unable to acknowledge their behaviour and attempt to change it.

Why?

The inability of someone to admit to or take responsibility for their actions means things never change. The cruel behaviour Frank suffered as a small child, giving Frank the message that he was not good enough for his father, plus the general ignorance of his condition, could have been when Frank's defence mechanisms were first adopted. Frank potentially displays a weakness, as he is never able to acknowledge this behaviour. Throughout life, Frank's 'denial and needing to be right, often bordering on abuse' tells us Frank was adopting these defences to make himself feel better and survive in a very stressful situation, a negative survival, as it can alienate him from other people even more.

Carl also was unable to acknowledge his behaviour. Jilly finally goes for divorce but we do not hear of Carl challenging this in any way, or attempting to acknowledge what happened. 'I couldn't get Carl to talk about it, he just got nasty.' Carl moves out. We do not know exactly what 'got nasty' means, but whatever it means, it indicates Carl was in denial, avoiding acknowledgement of the situation.

Ian also behaves in this way. Jilly tells us that when she tries to talk about problems, he says 'I can't remember'. She also gives us further examples of his behaviour: 'Not in an aggressive way, but just denial. As far as he was concerned it either never happened, wasn't quite like that, or was someone else's fault.' All these behaviours are defence mechanisms to avoid the truth.

Joe demonstrates a weakness in being unable to face his drink problem and get help to make the family life secure, 'he wasn't strong enough; the drink won,' Jilly tells us.

His denial of the situation is apparent from the statement 'with Joe hoping I might change my mind and turn a blind eye.' He loses his family in the process, and as Jilly realises, no one is able to do it for him; he is the one who needs to seek the help.

All these behaviours are defence mechanisms used by people unable to face their behaviour or take responsibility for it, and they can be frustrating and often infuriating for the person trying to initiate a way forward. Many clients come with this problem, being unable to understand why a family member or partner is behaving in this way. They often refuse to accompany the client to any sessions, or they make various excuses to ensure that they never actually attend any.

Other defence behaviours are lying, accusing the other person of the behaviour, saying nothing at all, refusing to talk at all, and trying to change the subject.

What people are actually saying by employing these behaviours is 'I don't want to talk about it.' If we can listen to this then we can start to feel less frustrated and it can start to make sense. But what do we do then? Nothing is going to get resolved or change! People with this defensive personality can be impossible to relate to healthily. Everything is fine until something goes wrong, when there is a problem with their behaviour. The more we push them to acknowledge reality, the more they can fight us on it, and things can get worse in the argument. Theoretically anyone can change behaviour if they want to, but not everyone is able to. Some people shy away from facing negative behaviour. Sometimes we have to accept that some people are just like that.

Traits of Personality

The two personality traits that surface repeatedly during my work with clients are the selfish and the caring. Caring trait people have to be very careful as very often they are not putting caring into themselves as well; it can be all about other people and their energy can get depleted. Also this kind of person can suddenly find themselves in a relationship with someone who has a selfish trait, if they are not seeing to their own needs. This is a common problem that is brought to me. When a caring trait person who is not caring for themselves meets a selfish trait person, the unconscious signals can go out in the following way: 'It doesn't matter about me, I never listen to myself, I always do what other people want.' This is the perfect signal for the selfish trait person to pick up, and out goes their signal: 'It's all about me, I won't be listening to you, I need someone who does what I want.' They match perfectly, though not truly of course as one of them is going to be very unhappy.

As long as we balance our lives and care about ourselves as well as others, we will attract like-minded people. Both giving and receiving creates a balanced, happy life. People can get great pleasure from giving, and if we do not allow this, or just don't expect it, we are not allowing the other person to get this pleasure.

Negative Ways of Escaping

'It was as if he gave up and nothing mattered anymore,' Jilly is told at her grandfather George's funeral. This is evidence that after the years of build-up, George maybe did eventually suffer from depression. It is sad to hear of his previously very successful business collapsing as he eventually loses the motivation for life that he had in the past. Tim Cantopher, a psychiatrist, wrote *Depressive Illness – The Curse of the Strong*, and indeed it is only the strong that can push themselves to these limits.

Jilly's mother tells her that George's drinking started after he returned from World War Two, and this also coincided with the children having grown up, so his family life with the demand for his support had gone. Left with an unhappy home life with his wife, and more time to think and feel about the past, his nightly alcohol consumption, giving temporary relief, would not have helped depression. Feeling better in the moment of the alcohol drinking, as the feelings are dulled and the company is an escape, it is hours later that the depressive qualities of alcohol consumption kick in. Alcohol itself is a depressant, and seeking more alcohol to dull this can result in a cycle of depressive and destructive behaviour.

The terrible shock for the family of discovering George's affair through a television news report is a double whammy. It was a shock in itself to discover the affair, but made worse for a family who ignores and denies negative things as here it is for the nation to see. In theory George would have been ripe for this kind of behaviour. In a marriage where there is no communication, no relationship, no physical time spent together over many years, it would just need the right person to come along and an affair can start. Bring alcohol into the mix and there's even more chance. Alcohol can cause us to lose our inhibitions, which means we are more out of control. Doing and saying things we do not normally do or say can be the hallmark of the drug alcohol. The phrase 'It's the drink talking' could be replaced with 'It's the part that never dares express it' talking. George is drinking every night, for many years. Ellen wanted to leave him at the point of the affair, but her daughters persuade her not to. Once more, Ellen is influenced by a familiar desire: to preserve the status quo. Here are her two daughters putting what looks best, first. The divorce laws were changing, and she could have left him anyway, with Harry by her side. She could have been firm with her daughters, but it was not familiar territory for her. Putting what looks best before what's actually best is the way she was brought up – it's the way she knows. If she had been of a different personality she may have stood up to her daughters. She reverts to her childhood teaching, does what her daughters want, and soldiers on for another fifteen years until George dies and she gets her 'happy release'.

'I don't know how people ever find time to have affairs,' said a friend of mine, back in the days of small children plus work. The thing about sexual attraction is that it can be a very strong force. A way will always be found because of this strong drive. Nature wants us to get together to mate, otherwise there will be no more humans. That is why people will risk and often lose important careers and whole families, devastate their children – because of this very strong life force.

To use an affair to escape an unhappy marriage is a negative way of coping. The unhappy marriage is still there, and the affair can bring more stress. To face the problems in the marriage and get help to work with them, to finally reach a positive change, or a decision to end, is the way that can bring eventual happiness.

Having Relationships

With a father unable to connect emotionally, and a withdrawn mother who has invested her emotional relationship in her son, Jilly's place in the family unit would have been an isolated one. It is this emotional isolation that can cause the neediness which surfaces within sexual relationships, and this reflects Jilly's hasty choice and attractions to partners who are not ultimately good for her.

Marrying Carl to escape home, becoming pregnant with Daisy soon after her divorce, before she and Joe have begun a future together – there had been no time for courting in either relationship, or getting to know the person better. Marrying Ian because he wanted to shows Jilly not listening to herself; what did *she* want? All these situations show neediness, unawareness, and an ignorance of her own thoughts and wishes.

There are familiar negative family traits in all three of Jilly's partners.

Jilly says she is in love with Carl, and then with Joe, 'I was in love again'. The feeling of being in love and the chemistry of sexual attraction and connection that it brings can be very strong, but unfortunately is often not enough to build a successful relationship and marriage. Who am I in love with? What kind of personality do they have? Are there any warning signs? Is there any negative behaviour? Even if we know the answers, they can be easy to ignore when we are in love.

A warning sign for Jilly comes in the early days of her relationship with Carl. When they visit his family home and Carl's mother is screaming at them to go away, Carl says, 'They're always like that,' indicating this is part of normal life for him. This is a warning sign as it tells us the type of behaviour Carl is used to, so it could be repeated by him, or any feelings carried from it could affect the relationship. It is a shock to Jilly who has bonded with Carl's family, indicating Carl has not talked openly about his family life to her.

Another warning sign for Jilly can be seen in relation to Joe. Joe is 'always down the pub,' sometimes calling in for a chat on the way there. He is not calling in at the pub on the way to see Jilly, which suggests the pub is the more important. If Jilly had been more secure and confident in herself as a deserving person, she would have felt this. If Jilly had also known more about alcoholism then she would have felt the negative of this situation, and visiting the pub every night was very familiar behaviour to her from her childhood days with her granddad.

Jilly realises she met Joe at a vulnerable time, very soon after her divorce and when she was struggling with Tom and her own feelings, experiencing the loss of both grandmothers.

Joe displays the familiar behaviour of Jilly's grandfather George, being a pub man, out every night. The fresh start he promised is not realised, as he continues his drinking behaviour. When Jilly's security with her children is threatened it becomes a turn-off and she ends the relationship.

To address the alcohol problem as a priority, before planning any future, would have given Jilly more of an idea of who Joe was, and how life might be with him. She didn't give herself a chance to get to know him properly, and was unable to recognise or feel the negativity of the pub behaviour at the start – or maybe she did and ignored it.

Jilly is close to her grandmothers but they are probably ultimately also at fault to some degree, as they are employing the family strategies too – notably with the denial of Frank's negative behaviour. She has many friends, and finds the genuineness and openness she seeks in the outside world, eventually going forward with friends and work colleagues to personal fulfillment. What she learns through her work gradually helps her in her own life and relationships. If we do not share parts of ourselves with loved ones, and friends who we can trust, our relationships are not intimate ones.

Jilly remembers her grandmother's story about how she lived within a marriage she felt was a mistake. Divorce is possible now of course, and there is a high rate in the Western world. However, with all the opportunities to end an unhappy situation, many people do not.

The best example of bonding and so being unable to leave is the domestic violence situation, where despite what are often terrible circumstances the victim stays in the relationship. The behaviour can be familiar and the bonds are the same as in a healthy relationship. Jilly tells us how she learns this in her training. The person stays when they should be running for the hills. Nature is not complicated. Nature doesn't say, 'Ooh, that won't be good for you so best not go there.' Nature says, 'It's what you know, so you'll feel comfortable with that.' Nature needs us to get together to mate, and it seems the more things we have in common from where we come from, the stronger the attraction. If we ignore what is happening to us, it seems that each subsequent relationship can produce more extreme behaviour.

A lot of my work has involved not only female victims of domestic violence but also male. I tried to start a male victims' support group in the past but none of them would come forward. There was still the stigma of feeling a failure, a fear of others finding out, and a fear of ridicule for continually being the victim of a woman's violence. With the childhood experiences it can work in exactly the same way for males as it does for females. At the time of writing there are no refuges for men; many I have worked with were sleeping in cars.

Even in later times, it is apparent from Jilly's story that working on a relationship instead of divorcing was not at that time a familiar concept. We have a higher profile for this now, with relationship counselling well publicised, and relationships can be worked on to change things for the better. This takes two people to work at it however, and if one partner is in denial, is unable to look at their behaviour, acknowledge 'bad stuff' or refuses to attend any helping environment, then the changes will not occur, no matter how much the other partner is putting in. It is then decisions would need to be made, to stay or go. Some people still spend years in unhappy relationships, never leaving, eventually one partner dying and the other living a lonely life of regret.

The sexual relationships in these stories are heterosexual. In my work with both gay and lesbian relationships and marriage, I have found there is little difference. The problems are all very similar.

The Most Important Relationship

Finally, Jilly discovers a happy relationship with herself by being able to live alone. One theory says we should all live alone at some time in our lives, to build a relationship with ourselves. Living alone doesn't mean being lonely. We all need connection with people: a close friend, others to chat with, the company of like-minded people, pursuing the fulfilling things we love to do. There can be nothing more lonely than a bad marriage or unhappy live-in partner relationship. We do not theoretically need to be in a live-in sexual relationship. We can have many choices available to us today, unlike in the past. For example, many people I have worked with are in happy relationships but in their own living accommodation. Getting to know oneself, one's likes and dislikes, giving ourselves what we want and need, means we then take a special strength into any relationship we have as we truly know who we are, and the other person will be able to get to know us properly. More importantly we know we can be happy on our own, so if things do go wrong we're not afraid to leave and so won't force ourselves to stay in an unhappy environment.

A relationship with ourselves is the most important relationship we will ever make, as the way we think and feel about ourselves has a big influence on the kind of people we will attract into our lives. It is also the most secure as we will never leave!

Family Patterns

The main pattern in this family as we go through the generations is held emotion, or suppressed emotion: feelings are being held inside and not expressed.

We see the results of suppressed emotion in behaviour and in physical ailments.

Mary has been brought up in an environment where her father George is described as withdrawn and doesn't share his feelings or problems with anyone. Mary's mother Ellen previously described her mother as withdrawn, so this trait in George would have been familiar to Ellen. She may not have felt it as negative to start with, even if she was aware of it, but as a familiar, comfortable place to be. When Mary meets Frank, he is not withdrawn; she is the one who is withdrawn. Frank however will have an inability to emotionally connect, so this can at first feel comfortable to Mary as it is basically familiar to her, and can also feel safe, as her emotions are out of sight too, but for different reasons. There are many similarities between the generations, and as we go through we are reminded of a previous person. See how many you can spot.

We can break negative behaviour patterns in our families by recognising them, disagreeing with them, and then doing it differently. The way Frank is with daughter Jilly on their family holidays is a good example of a parent consciously choosing to do it differently, as he remembers his own 'agony' on holidays as a boy.

Learning from the past is something we can all do, and we can pass our learning on to others. No past experiences need be a waste of time; they can help us change what we do to make our lives better. An example of learning from the past is when Jilly leaves Ian, saying she is not going to have any repetitions of her past. She leaves, so Daisy is protected.

There is a theory that we either do things exactly the same as our families, without thinking about it, or we do it completely differently, determined not to repeat it. It is personality and growth that

133

dictate which way we go. If we want to keep an eye on our own lives then awareness is the first step, and then after that to be able to recognise a negative behaviour when we see it, both in ourselves and in others. Remember, we only need one incident to tell us what a person does. It is also very important to value ourselves. The signal we need to put out is that we are worth loving.

Changing It

In the early days of these stories, personal therapy would not have been heard about. Even Jilly, working on a helpline, says that she never heard about people going for professional help for relationship problems, and that looking back, she treated her solicitor like a counsellor.

Any behaviour can be changed in theory, but only if the person exhibiting the behaviour wants to change it. It can be hard work to change something we have been programmed to do, or something we have been doing for many years. Those pathways of thinking in the brain will be very strong.

'Going out there and practising it, that's the hardest part,' said a client. Yes, I can give you the tools, but you are the one who has to go out there and use them, over and over again until it becomes your natural way – and it does, time and time again.

To change we need awareness of what we are doing, a desire to change it, and maturity to accept responsibility for it. 'I do that because my father did' is OK in itself and probably true, but that is no reason to not change. We can make conscious decisions to change what we do.

If we have had a particularly tough time, we may need help to do this. Therapy is a safe place to explore the self and gain the tools for change. One of the conditions of my training as a therapist was to receive a minimum of twenty hours' personal therapy. It can be a life-changing experience and for me, I gained a lot of insight into myself and my behaviour; I learned techniques for change, and was able to rid myself of some old personal feelings. It certainly made a difference in helping me relate to clients, as I had to be prepared for any personality to be walking through the door.

A good start to finding a suitable counsellor or psychotherapist is word of mouth. If this is impossible then a professionally qualified therapist should carry insurance and belong to a governing body. However, the most important factor is our relationship with the therapist. We should be able to feel comfortable, that we can trust this person and feel accepted. If these conditions are not present, we may not be able to talk freely and discharge all that we want and need to, and then the therapy may not work for us. If we are paying, then we need to get a good service like we would with any other industry. If we went to a hairdresser and came out feeling uncomfortable, or that something wasn't right because they didn't listen to what we wanted, it is unlikely we would go back again. The same applies to a therapist. Shop around if you need to: maybe try out different ones, until you find a person who feels right for you.

The past generations in this book did not have this opportunity. Frank with Asperger's Syndrome lived in a time where this condition was not common knowledge and he struggled, building up his defences in the process, as did many. George and Ellen made the best of what they had, working hard through their lives, and living through their family. Once the family had gone, George negatively escaped feelings and home life through drink. Ellen clung on to her youngest son, unable to face the prospect of having no children at home.

People like Will (the uncle who never spoke), and Mary and Harry with their learned way of suppressing feelings, would not have found it easy to change without help. Coming from a background where talking openly is discouraged can make it very difficult to relate closely and openly to others in adulthood.

If we feel we want to change our life and attract different people into it, then we need to acknowledge our own background and work to heal any hurts we may have from that time. It is important to see yourself in a genuine way, and not through the eyes of any negative care you may have received, either psychological or physical. By acknowledging any bad caring, we are not 'slagging someone off' as one client said they felt they were doing, but just being honest and genuine about our past.

The role of the family for a lot of the people I meet in my work can be damaging and destructive. The important thing about growing up is that we then have a choice. As a child we have to stay where we are, and our personal power is limited. As an adult there is no need to stay in any environment that is unhealthy for us. The world is full of healthy places and people for us to discover.

We have a great opportunity in our society today to receive support and guidance, and change the things we wish to change.

Toolbox

Caring For Yourself

It can be surprising how many wonderful carers and support workers are ignoring their own needs and putting themselves into negative personal relationships, eventually suffering from stress and other problems, caused by the build-up of self-neglect over the years.

Have you ever spent time doing nothing? 'Huh! Chance would be a fine thing!' 'Goodness no, that sounds very boring!' Actually, doing nothing is one of the healthiest things you can do for yourself.

Doing nothing has different meanings for different people and finding what is right for you is important. Listening to music, watching DVDs, snoozing, staring into space thinking, staring into space not thinking, pottering around the house, walking on the beach or in the woods, sitting in silence, spending a day alone, writing in a diary or journal. All these activities have been related by clients when I have questioned their statement 'I did nothing that day', or 'I haven't done anything this morning', but all were activities they enjoyed and found relaxing. Your mind needs to recharge from time to time and it cannot do that if it has constant stimulation and demand. One of the great stress busters is 'doing nothing'. Planning and making a date with yourself can help to give you the time that you need. If you have children, getting someone to mind the kids for a couple of hours, half a day, a whole day, a weekend; maybe a partner, a friend, doing a minding exchange, or paying a minder can give you that time. This has to be done without guilt. It is good for your children's social development to relate to others. Human babies are able to bond with more than one person, one of the reasons we have survived so well as a species, so any fears you may have of losing that bond are unfounded. Letting go of things that don't matter, refusing an invitation if it feels like a chore; there are many ways we can treat ourselves more kindly.

Caring for oneself means listening to the self to make sure we get what we need. Giving yourself time and listening to yourself will counteract stress, and help you to find a fulfilling life. Listening to ourselves means listening to the thoughts that come into our head about what we might feel we need. 'I'm so tired, I need an early night' or 'I need some quiet for myself' can be met with an opposing thought, like an authoritarian voice saying 'You can't do that! That would be lazy/ wrong/ you have to do this/ you have to do that!' It is surprising how badly we can treat ourselves by not only ignoring our own needs, but also by being quite hostile to them. If you think about it you (hopefully!) wouldn't treat someone else like this. What you want or need cannot always be met straight away but we can make a date or a promise with ourselves to do it. If we were parented in a negative way, we can find we are treating ourselves in the same way. Or we may have had a role model of someone who pushes themselves to great limits, so we find we are doing the same.

Anger

Carried feelings from the past need to be released, and anger is often one of the strongest of those. Finding someone to express these feelings with, or writing them down using any language or drawing pictures, can enable the self to feel lighter. If the feelings are very strong and you have questions that you need answers to, you may need to find professional help.

A lot of people have problems with anger, seeing it as something 'bad' that we shouldn't be feeling. Anger is just another feeling or emotion that tells us something is wrong. It is what we do with the anger that is important. Keeping it inside us can be damaging for the body. Psychological diagnosis often relates to anger stored in the body (unexplained back pain as was the case for Harry), and carried anger is one of the common reasons for depression, which Harry also suffered with in later life.

Anger can be a huge energy that has the ability to manifest in a physical way, and it takes a lot of resources to carry that around. If this is the way a person copes with it, then over time the anger will build up, draining the energy resources, until the psyche says, 'No more, I can't cope,' and starts to shut down, resulting in depressive symptoms. Non-motivation, lack of energy, and in its extreme form, not understanding what other people are saying, a frightening situation to be in, are all signs of depression to varying degrees.

We read in the news of someone described by his shocked neighbours as a quiet, mild-mannered person, a lovely family man, and then go on to read how he suddenly killed his whole family. Why? A massive amount of suppressed anger bursting out all at once, resulting in a terrible tragedy, that is one reason, and that is what anger can do. Of course these events are extremely rare, which is why they make the news, but this is what can happen with suppressed anger. It can suddenly burst out during some trivial situation, at best shocking those who witness it and at worst leading to damage, injury, and death.

Anger is an energy and should be used in a positive way.

Jilly carried anger towards her parents; she tells us how she had sessions of personal therapy where she dealt with these feelings, to understand them and release them. Jilly was carrying feelings inside, the way her mother did. With Mary's own behaviour and attempts to suppress Jilly's natural exuberance as a child, Jilly could easily have adopted this family way. It is a good example of repeating learned behaviour without thinking about it. She tells us how she realises later that she has done this when she remembers saying nothing in response to Carl's outbursts. Because she is different from her mother, she seeks out ways to get what she needs, instead of holding things inside of herself forever. Both Carl and George are carriers of anger from the past and are discharging it negatively through expression to others.

One of the ways we work with anger is to discharge it positively.

If a person finds difficulty talking and expressing themselves, I encourage them to write it down, keep a journal, a private book for themselves, to use whatever words they need, and drawing pictures too if that is expressive for them. It helps to get the anger out of their head and into the book. 'Getting it out of my head and onto paper,' said a client, 'I feel so much lighter.' Sometimes it can bring up more feelings as they read it back to themselves, or look at the expressive pictures they constructed. We can acknowledge here again how some people find writing does not come easily to them but they can use pictures and diagrams instead, and as before there is no judgment on what is written or drawn, it just needs to feel expressive for the self.

Another writing tool is what we call 'a therapy letter'. Writing a letter to the person we have a problem with, saying all the things we need to say to them, using whatever words we feel we need to, can be a very releasing experience. The idea is not to post it, but of course we can, and some have. Because of this we can also address a person who has died with our anger. The purpose is to rid ourselves of all the strong anger energy. If we do send it to the person we are angry with, we must be prepared for non-acknowledgement, denial, blame, or no response at all. The person knows what they've done, but they're not necessarily going to take any responsibility for it; very often it's just not worth the stamp! It is important we feel in control, as built up anger can stem from family life where things were unfair for us as a child, and we had no control over our own life. We are not making any excuses for a perpetrator when we explain behaviour. As a child we have a right to be angry with anyone who has failed us, damaged us, cruelly treated us, and we can have a need to express this anger as an adult. As an adult we have the right to understand why our carers fail us.

As more angry feelings come up another healthy way to release them is physically. Not everyone has the space to hang a punch bag, but punching the bed is a very good substitute. No damage to the self (punching a wall) or others (punching a person) or objects (smashing things, kicking through doors), by vigorous punching of the bed. Maybe imagining it is the person we are angry with will help, and however many years ago the anger stems from, this can be a very positive therapeutic experience. Punching walls or people, destroying objects or worse, can harm the self physically, and also may cause police arrest.

As with generally discharging stress, the tools for anger are the same. The idea is to just keep on discharging, thumping the bed or the couch, or if we have the resources a punch bag, whenever we need to. Regular discharge by positive physical release can help in the day-to-day management of any angry feelings and any physical activity can help. It is important to find one that suits you best. Some people like to visit the gym, others love walking or jogging. I always enjoy a long, peaceful swim. A friend of mine plays table tennis; another plays squash.

Another physical way to release anger is shouting and screaming. Not everyone feels the need for this, but many do. Worrying about upsetting the neighbours or loved ones, the need can be kept inside. One client would drive to a deserted spot, shut all the car windows and scream and rant inside. The deserted spot may be the answer even without a car, and hopefully a date can be made with the self to achieve this.

Talking to the person we are angry with can resolve anger feelings. Thinking 'discussion' instead of 'argument' can help, and explaining how we feel and why gives the other person a chance to communicate with us. However, not everyone can do this healthily and if we feel it is not a good idea to confront someone, maybe it is our boss at work and we feel our job might be jeopardised, for example, or maybe it's someone who we know is prone to violence, or maybe it's someone who is not in our lives anymore, then we can find someone we can trust to talk about it with and vent our feelings.

All these tools are ways of living with anger as we go through life, as we all at some time will encounter it; it is a normal human emotion.

Apart from all these tools, what really seems to create a huge shift in an angry person is understanding where all the anger comes from, and why. This usually involves understanding a person, people, or situation, which may have been responsible for that anger. I prefer to use the word 'acceptance' rather than 'forgiveness'.

Once this awareness and understanding is reached, the person can display a calmness not seen previously. 'It is like a window has been opened,' remarked one client, 'I can now see clearly.' Travelling back in time to examine what was going on in our childhood and our past relationships can be a very healing process. It means that the person doing the travelling will at last get an answer to the question they have often been carrying for years: 'Why?'

Grieving

We haven't been very good at grieving in our society, although we are getting better. 'Don't mention it, she might cry.' 'I don't know what to say to him.' 'She keeps crying, I think she's having a breakdown.' 'I made sure I didn't cry at the funeral.'

In some other cultures it's the norm for the grieving to wail in order to express their emotion. A good example of healthy grieving is in the Buddhist culture where ritual grieving can last a week or more. The village provides food for the family, who are then able to concentrate on the person they have lost, and wailing and crying are accepted as normal. Much time can be spent in the temple with the body, which is finally cremated. Various rituals are performed, a boat may be hired, and the ashes scattered with rose petals over water, the monks present with the family. Crying, wailing and generally grieving is expected at this time. It is a process that helps the coming to terms with the physical loss of the person, and enables the release of feelings. Crying is a release and should never be stopped. If we feel we want to cry and it is an inappropriate place, then we need to make a date with ourselves to concentrate on the issue and cry as much as we want to. A weekly date can be good for someone still affected by a death years ago. If we don't allow ourselves to grieve, the feelings are still held inside. Sometimes the death of someone else can trigger past feelings of grief. We could find ourselves weeping for a deceased person we never knew, as those held feelings are felt once more. There is no time limit for grieving; the closer the relationship, the more feelings to release, the longer to accept. If we allow the process without criticism or limitation, then gradually the way we think and feel will change. It is not about forgetting the person, it is about changing the way we feel about it from those early, strong and sometimes unbearable feelings. We need to expect all sorts of feelings when we are going through the grieving process. Anger is a common one, anger that the person has gone, feeling angry with the person for going, however irrational this may seem. Whatever the feelings are, it is important we allow ourselves to feel them, to understand them and to release them.

The relationship is the crux for how the grieving manifests, and if there was no close relationship then the grieving can be far less; sometimes there is nothing to grieve. Jilly briefly tells how her mother died, in contrast to feelings expressed and more details when her grandmothers died. It is possible to feel nothing, to be unmoved when a person we have known all our lives dies – even a parent. Not the nothingness or numbness of feelings that can come with grief, but a genuine untouched feeling, like a stranger we never knew has died. Even if there was no relationship and so nothing to grieve, tremendous guilt can manifest in some people when this happens. Am I uncaring? Am I a horrible person? What's wrong with me? There is nothing wrong. If the relationship was not a close one, or maybe it was even an abusive one, the feelings of closeness have not been developed or felt, then there is nothing to miss, so there is nothing to grieve.

Guilt

Tom stays with his dad when Jilly moves to Norfolk; she thinks things have changed and everything will be all right as Carl's environment is less stressful. However this is a huge risk, as when a person behaves in a certain way it tells us this is what they are capable of, and the behaviour can materialise again at any time, given the right conditions. Carl has not demonstrated taking any responsibility for his behaviour, by acknowledging it or attempting to change it. We hear this when Jilly tells us she starts to stick up for herself, and Carl's behaviour then gets worse. When she tries to talk about it, 'he just got nasty'.

Jilly still carries feelings from that time when she left Tom behind: the feelings of guilt. In therapy we work to change the thought. 'Left Tom behind' could be changed to 'allowed Tom to stay', which is a much truer statement, and helps Jilly to recognise how she was thinking of Tom at the time. To remember we are human and not perfectly programmed robots is a very common activity during therapy, helping to acknowledge that the person did the best they could at the time, and hindsight can put a different angle on it, as we now have knowledge we didn't have in the past. Jilly would need to recognise she was being the good parent she was, always trying to make things better, and as parents we can't do more than that. Putting unreasonable demands on oneself is unfair. We are human, therefore we will make mistakes. Anyone trying to be generally perfect in life is in theory going to fail. Mistakes are an opportunity for learning, and can be used to go forward and do things differently in the future, or we can use our experiences to help others. This is how we grow as people.

Another type of guilt that can be carried is someone else's guilt. This is common in an abusive situation, where someone has been raped, where there has been childhood neglect, where someone is displaying the selfish trait. The strong caring personality easily takes on the guilt, with the ability to look at their behaviour they start to think, 'If only I'd done this or that it would have been all right.' The guilt lies with the perpetrator and in therapy, we visualise handing it back to them.

An eldest child in a family who is of a caring and responsible personality will easily take on the role of protector, or parent, to the younger siblings in an environment with irresponsible carers, abuse, neglect or cruelty. Many years later this person can look back and criticise themselves for not doing better, for not protecting or changing the situation. We then look at the reality, that this person was also a child who was suffering in the environment, and should have had the protection and nurturing all children should have. Again, the guilt is with the perpetrator and we 'hand it back'.

Although it is not in the stories, I will mention the ultimate result of suppression, which can also result in much guilt. The story of a partner or child who has committed suicide, and the partner or parent who is left behind and eaten away with the guilt that they didn't spot the signs, or prevent the act, is a common one.

A person who wants to commit suicide can go to extreme lengths to make sure no one knows. They want to do it, and they know they will be stopped. We have to try to understand that very black despairing place where people who commit suicide can find themselves. They are often very good at hiding it too, appearing quite their normal selves on the outside. It is a very sad situation as the person who commits suicide often feels there is no way out, but in theory there is always a way out. Guilt is worked with in therapy by understanding the other person's behaviour and recognising it was what they wanted at the time, allowing the guilt to dissipate, and once again we have to accept and allow ourselves to be human.

Worry

The trouble with us humans can be that we have such amazing imaginations. All the wonderful creativity that we can witness in the world that stems from the human creative brain is evidence of this. The trouble with it is that this fabulous creativity can be used in a negative way, by worrying. When we worry, we are busy using our wonderful imagination but in a very negative way. 'What if?' is a common question. 'What if I miss the train?' 'What if I can't pay the bill?' 'What if I get ill?' 'What if she fails her exam?' 'What if I don't get the job?' Our creativity can be so good, we can feel the worst has already happened and using our imagination to create negative scenes, we are suffering the feelings that go with it.

Instead of being stuck in imagining the worst, we can first use our imagination to create what we would do if the worst did happen. There may be several possibilities here. For example: what if I miss the train? I will get a taxi, I will phone my friend, I will go the next day, I will wait for the next one, I will go another time, or I will plan an alternative route. Once we have made a plan, we can even write it down and put it away in a drawer, we can then tell ourselves we've done all we can. We then recognise that thinking about this any more is pointless as we have no idea what is eventually actually going to happen (although we might think we do) and thinking the worst is not going to change anything.

If we find ourselves thinking about this particular worry again, we can recognise it and immediately switch our thoughts to something else. The 'something else' will be something nice that we have decided to use in place of the worry, like a holiday we would like, planning a favourite meal or night out. It needn't be a true thought that we are actually going to do, it can be a fantasy thought. After all, most worries are fantasy thoughts. The reality can usually prove very different.

Planning ahead what thought we are going to use means we can switch immediately without allowing the worry thought to take hold. It may not be easy to start with, but just remembering that the original thought is in the drawer and you have done all you can with that at the moment can help.

If we can catch ourselves worrying and immediately recognise what we are doing with our wonderful imagination and what a waste of energy it is, and also drain of energy, then this can be enough to get us on the road to change.

But we have to work at it.

Realising that the past has gone and we are now free can be liberating and life-changing. As children we are powerless in the way we have to be in certain places and with certain people, and generally we do not have choices, but that all changes when we grow up, when we can choose who to have in our lives and where to be. Unfortunately a lot of people still feel and behave like they did when they were children and feel powerless, repeating the patterns from childhood. Acknowledge the personal power and remember we have many different parts to ourselves; talk to that part of you that hasn't caught up yet and is still in the past. Reassure that part of you, talk to it out loud if necessary, let it know you are in charge now, you are the strong adult who will protect it and not allow the negative in, will defend it, listen to it and take it into positive environments.

Head Sorting

If you have lots of demands in your head that cause you to feel stressed, give you difficulty sleeping, or generally stop you from being in the moment and enjoying life then there are things you can do to take charge.

Get the tasks or demands out of your head and write them down on a piece of paper. Now look at them and prioritise in order of importance.

Look at them again and see if there are any you can cross off.

Recognise whether you are being demanding or critical of

yourself, and try to be kinder and help yourself to 'let go' of certain demands, to ask for help, or delegate. Remember you are not solely responsible for everything, you will not always be able to achieve everything, as you are human and not a robot that can be programmed for perfection, so you will also sometimes make mistakes – use them for learning.

Look at your list again, which hopefully may be shorter this time, or contain fewer demands. Ask yourself, 'If I don't do this task this week will it matter?' or 'If I don't do this task at all will it matter?' Try to 'let go' of demands and recognise if the demand is coming from the past. 'If I sit down, I hear my father's voice saying "Come on don't be lazy, see it through"!' said a client. If you recognise someone else's beliefs, tell them in your head they are out of date now and this is how it is going to be. Trust yourself to know what is best for you. The person that does the demanding is not doing it the healthy way.

It's always a good idea to write down thoughts or lists of things you want to do or remember. If you do this, you won't need to carry them around in your head and your mind is freed up for creativity.

Mind and Body

We hear how Mary suffered various psychological ailments: 'The loss of taste she had for five years before she told me.' Mary's inward personality and her learned behaviour, resulting in her keeping her problems to herself, means she is carrying a lot of negative feelings. Mary is not releasing this by stress reaction directed at the family like her father, but holding everything inside herself, which eventually starts attacking her body, resulting in psychological ailments.

Harry, Mary's brother, also dealt with feelings this way leading to years of back pain originating from psychological causes. Growing apart from the parent is a natural process and separation is healthy.

The relationship is re-established on an adult footing as time goes by. A needy and controlling parent who wants to keep the child to themselves, fearing a void if the child leaves, can result in the child carrying a lot of anger which can be held inside, sometimes so deep he or she can be unaware of it. Guilt can also be carried as the child tries to live up to expectations at the expense of his own needs, and fulfill those of the mother.

A double guilt can manifest, as the child fails to fulfill his own life too. As well as being his mother's close relationship, Harry was the youngest child out of all the four children who, when eventually left behind, would have witnessed the unspoken tensions and pain between his parents. Being in a group of siblings can buffet and protect to a certain extent, but Harry was eventually alone with his parents to fully absorb the tense environment, and apart from periods of working away, it was for almost the rest of his life. There can also be hostility from the father in these situations, spoken or unspoken, when the son is the prime close connection to the mother, depending on the father's personality. Shocked at her Uncle Harry's eventual bent figure, Jilly says it's like he is carrying the world, and he was certainly carrying a lot, with his parents relationship, and his own life on hold.

Another example of mind and body connection is the case of a client who was referred for psychological help. In her forties and working in a care home, Joan had been to the doctors for many years with a 'lost voice'. Her voice was very husky and quiet as if she had a bad throat, but the hospital tests over seven years had indicated nothing physically wrong. A communication problem was discovered with her mother. A verbally and emotionally abusive childhood had resulted in Joan being powerless where her mother was concerned and even in adulthood she was still enduring abuse as she continued her relationship with her mother.

Uncomplaining, accepting this situation as normal and never speaking about it, Joan was still helping her mother with shopping and other activities, responding to her mother's selfish demands at the expense of her own life. By recognising what had happened to her and what was still happening, Joan was able to understand her situation and make empowering changes to her life and relationships. By gradually trying out new techniques of communication, and recognising and accepting her mother's personality, Joan's confidence grew, her life changed and after about a year, her voice returned.

Any unexplained ailments may originate with what we may be holding inside. Are we afraid to express anger? Are we afraid of anger generally? Have we done things we regret and do we carry guilt? Are we carrying someone else's guilt? Have we experienced tragedy and not allowed ourselves to feel? Have we experienced loss and not allowed ourselves to grieve?

All these situations can be worked with to reach understanding and acceptance, releasing feelings, learning new techniques, to go forward in a happier life that is right for us.

Alternative Therapies

There are many different alternative therapies. Massage, reflexology (foot massage), reiki, Indian head massage, spiritual healing and acupuncture, to name a few.

Generalising, in our western society we probably do not get enough touch. Studies have demonstrated the health benefits of touch. Some doctors' surgeries now offer massage, aromatherapy and reflexology on prescription, and my local baby clinic runs baby massage classes for new mums. We are a lot better than we used to be. People will hug a lot more now. 'I was never hugged, nobody touched, but when I went there everybody hugged!' said a lovely lady about a group she had joined. With positive touch we can get connection and calm, and receive some of the same benefits and more that we get from a relaxation exercise.

We can also give these benefits to each other. Sitting quietly in a comfortable chair, with maybe some relaxing music, slowing your breathing down, while the other person lays their hands gently on your shoulders for ten minutes can be a wonderful, calming experience.

Relaxation Exercise

This one is very easy and has proved very effective for getting to sleep, getting back to sleep, or relaxing the body to help strengthen the immune system.

Before you start the exercise you may have thoughts in your head that are difficult to get rid of. 'I mustn't forget to sort that out when I get into work.' 'I need to phone Sue.' 'I mustn't forget it's my turn to pick up the kids.' Any thoughts, write them down to get them out of your head and onto the paper. Put the paper with the written thoughts under the chair or bed, knowing that you can look at it when you have finished so you needn't try and remember them.

Put on some favourite relaxing music or have silence if preferred.

Sit well back in a comfortable chair with both feet on the floor, or lie down on a bed or sofa.

Start to breathe more slowly. You will find that as you consciously allow more time for one breath in and one breath out, you will automatically be breathing more deeply. Concentrate on this for a minute or two.

Now take your attention to your feet, be aware of them on the floor or the bed, slowly start to relax them, let them go. Flop them!

When this has been achieved, concentrate on your legs and do the same.

Moving up your body to your lower body, relax tummy muscles.

Then your upper body, becoming conscious of your breathing again and making sure it is still slowed down.

Your facial muscles next – relax.

Your shoulders – let them go.

Relax your arms down to your hands, which can flop in your lap or beside you.

Check your breathing again to make sure it is still slowed down. Your body should now be in a state of relaxation.

Achieving a state of relaxation can cause brain waves to become slower and deeper, decrease stress hormones as they are no longer being produced by the adrenal glands, decrease blood pressure and heart rate, decrease sweating, decrease muscle tension and strengthen the immune system.

While you have been doing this exercise you have been 'in the moment' (or should have been if you managed to write those thoughts down and put them away!) This being in the moment or being in the present can be a very stress-free place to be. Children operate in this way most of the time, but when we grow up and have demands on ourselves, we can forget how to do this. A lot of my training as a therapist involved practising being in the moment. I need to be in this mode when I am working with a client, or I may miss something crucial they are saying, but also they can feel it if I'm not with them, if my mind is somewhere else, even for a few seconds, and that can cause damage in the therapy process.

Next time you're out and about, see if you are in the present and aware of your surroundings. What can you can hear? Maybe birds singing, people talking, the wind in the trees, or maybe there is silence. Look around at what you can see: maybe the colours and types of buildings, trees and flowers, people, children playing, a lovely view. What can you feel? The wind on your face, the feeling or smell of the rain, the warmth of the sun, or the cold air. Very often we can physically be in one environment and mentally in another, and we can miss so much. We cannot always be in the present of course, we need to plan ahead, and we need to think of things past, to sort out our thoughts. Consciously allowing ourselves to be in the moment at certain times can lower our stress levels, and give us more pleasure in life.

Anger, grieving, guilt, worry, demands – all these if not dealt with will cause stress and stress behaviour. If we can deal with these situations by using the tools above we can make life easier and happier for ourselves, and according to current studies, live a longer life too. Stress is one of the main causes of premature death in the Western world.

The Transpersonal

Transpersonal therapy is concerned with being able to reach our highest ability, and to do this we can get in touch with an unconscious part of ourselves, which in transpersonal therapy and also within healing groups is called the 'higher self'.

Transpersonal therapy works with an unconscious knowing we all have. We can bring this knowing into consciousness by calming life down, creating a quiet personal space for ourselves, using relaxation exercises and meditation, ridding our minds of everyday thoughts. We are then open to answers and information that we cannot get when we are bogged down with everyday details and demands. This part of ourselves that we can reach called the 'higher self' knows what's best for us, knows our life journey and what we need, and can give us these moments of sudden insight, as certain thoughts arise in our head.

Some people in transpersonal counselling may use the words 'soul', 'spirit' or 'God' and some other people can find these words uncomfortable. People like Jilly in the time when she rejected the church of her upbringing could be an example of this. It is important we find our own words for the experience. Some people will reject the words 'higher self' and say the messages come from God; others will say they are from guides, or angels. Whatever we believe, the experience will be the same.

Jilly has a new experience after she leaves her healing group. 'I felt I was still there, in the group with them all, and I had the most wonderful feeling of love and belonging. I thought if everyone could experience this, no one would ever feel lonely.' In the group that evening, Jilly would have done the usual relaxations and meditations before giving and/or receiving healing. Her state of mind and body would have been open, and still in that meditative state of consciousness, she has a feeling of no boundaries, and a close inner connection. In healing groups, being open means the crown chakra or energy centre at the crown of the head can enable connection. The transpersonal way is advocated in healing groups too, through guided relaxation, meditation, and other exercises to get in touch with the higher self.

There have been many research papers published by the British Psychological Society's *Transpersonal Psychology Review*, and much has been written to forward the knowledge of this therapy.

Psychologist John Rowan is a strong advocate of transpersonal counselling. He and scientist Ken Wilber have worked to further develop the concept. Like the 'listening to self' tool but going a lot deeper into the mind and deeper into ourselves, transpersonal therapy enables us with practice to eventually be aware of how we really feel and what we truly need, and then eventually to act on this knowledge.

The ideas and decisions reached when in the transpersonal space can sometimes surprise and even amaze. As well as discovering more about ourselves and listening to our own thoughts, the transpersonal space has provided an outlet for personal creativity by making many people aware of their potential. We can then go forward to live our lives in the best way possible for ourselves. Creative thoughts and ideas can suddenly seem to come from nowhere in the transpersonal space.

The creative silence: creating the place for perceptive awareness. You will be giving your mind the opportunity to do what it is capable of doing.

Putting the Normal in Paranormal

What happens when we die? The answer to this is constantly being sought. People say they know what happens, governed by their faith. Others say they know what happens governed by their instincts. Who is right or wrong? They can all say they're right, they can all feel they're right, but no one knows, as there has never been any hard evidence. Or has there?

Those people born with a sense of 'seeing' – being able to see, sense, and hear what others cannot, will say yes, there is evidence; we see it, we hear it. But many ignore them, some through fear, some through their religion, and some through just not being able to accept what is being said.

'Paranormal' means crossing the boundaries of normal experience, but for many people these experiences are normal, something they have experienced as far back as they can remember, often a family trait shared and experienced together. But some have not shared. Brought up in families where denial is encouraged or even where aggression and abuse is directed against a child who tries to share what he or she is experiencing, many learn to suppress their experiences and some live in fear that they are 'going mad'.

I have come across many people during my life who have experienced the paranormal and many I have helped within my work as a therapist to accept themselves and acknowledge their special ability. By doing so, it will help them find like-minded people and recognise when they feel uncomfortable, when sharing is not appropriate for their own survival.

But has paranormal really got anything to do with life after death? You will have to reach your own conclusions after reading the experiences in this book, or maybe it will make you hungry to research more.

My Experiences

When I was a little girl from maybe two or three years old visiting my grandmother, I have a memory of not wanting to go upstairs by myself. It felt like there was 'something up there'. At seven years old I would rush up the stairs to go to the bathroom, shut the door, wee very quickly, and then rush down again, trying not to look at the bedroom doors or the landing area. I never saw anything but there was this very uncomfortable feeling bordering on fear. It was to be repeated almost thirty years later in another house which my mum and dad owned and where I had to spend the night alone. I was able to find an explanation for it from a spiritual therapist who said I had picked up the fear from my mother who she said could also sense things like this and felt it was frightening. I didn't know my mother had any experiences like this as she never said she did, probably because she didn't want to frighten me, but in the way all children can do, I was able to sense this unconsciously. The therapist told me where I was going wrong was that there was nothing to fear. I was just sensing, and it could be something from the past, or an energy that had been left behind. Experiences of the paranormal can be both interesting and fascinating. Some people will ridicule or deny them, but whole university departments are devoted to research in this field.

Apart from her own personal experiences, Jilly quotes various little stories she heard through life, and I too have heard these types of stories. A lot have come from my clients and I have found myself in a position to reassure, especially when the stories stem from a very young age. I was coming across so many paranormal cases within my work, eventually I did a training course in paranormal counselling.

One client, a young single mother suffering from anxiety, with no family support, was worried her feelings of stress were impacting on her ability to enjoy and care for her baby in the best way. I will call her Sarah.

At our fourth session, Sarah suddenly said 'I see a lady', then hurriedly correcting herself, 'I don't mean now, but I see a lady sometimes and I have always seen her, since I was about four years old.' I encouraged her to continue, and she told me that at first she would call this lady 'Mummy'.

'I thought she was my other mummy, but my real mother got cross and told me the lady wasn't there, so I stopped saying it out loud. She's been there all my life.'

I suddenly felt for that little girl who would have definitely felt she needed another mummy, as was obvious from Sarah's sad story of her past. The more we talked about it, the more relief was appearing over Sarah's face. I gave Sarah the various explanations, a psychological explanation that she was unconsciously creating another mother for herself as a survival technique, and how there are many people who 'see' and say they know the people they see are in another dimension or on 'the other side'.

'Thank God! I thought you were going to section me!'

(Sectioning: the compulsory detaining of a person who is diagnosed as being a danger to self and/or others.)

So now it was my turn to feel concern. 'Of course I'm not going to section you!' I said. 'There are many explanations for these things and many people experience the same as you.'

'No one else can ever see her! I thought I was mad!' she exclaimed. 'I've even thought I might get worse!'

Sarah had been keeping this to herself nearly all her life, fearing she may be mad or was going mad, needing to keep it hidden.

Sarah was interested and relieved to hear she was not alone in her experience and as she had been carrying these thoughts all her life, this was just another concern for her to shoulder along with all the other feelings of sadness, anger, guilt and anxiety.

Continually asking 'Who am I?' and worrying about getting 'worse' can result in low self-esteem, as well as being very stressful.

It didn't matter which explanation Sarah chose to believe and help to explain her experience, and I didn't need to know. She would choose the one that felt right for her.

During my time over years of work in the field of emotional support, more than one client has said to me 'I think I might be mad'. I started to realise how many people are born with a psychic ability and how for some of those people it can be a burden to carry.

One lovely lady I met who has spent a lot of her life helping others has seen 'paranormal people' ever since she was a young child. All the females in her family have had the same experience through several generations and it helps that they are able to talk about it together. They are greatly aware that other people do not have these experiences and because they may not be believed, or worse, thought to be 'mad', they are very careful with whom they share the information.

Another client, Carly, was struggling to cope with many problems involving family and relationships. She had a mother who was demanding and always talked about her own problems but never listened to Carly. She had a brother who was 'always a problem' and she had taken on a family role of being the one expected to sort everything out. Her partner was demanding and immature and she was shouldering the sole upbringing of the children.

She lived in a village with no transport so I visited her at home.

At each session she would offload a lot of feelings about the past and the present. We looked at ways she could change communication, look after herself, and think about ways to change her life for the future.

After about five sessions she shared it. 'It's when I sit at the kitchen table, I often do various work there, it's the only table we've got! I know it sounds weird but I keep feeling something touching my shoulder, someone is behind me, or it feels that they are, and I immediately think of my dad, every time!'

Carly's father had died five years earlier and they had been very close. When she started to talk about him, she felt he was actually the only person in her life that she had ever been close too, and who had really understood her. I explained to her the spiritualist theory, her father existing in another dimension, and then the psychological theory, part of herself unconsciously arranging this, as it's what she needs.

'I do feel he's here for me, and he's helping me too,' she said. 'I'm glad we've talked about it, I do find it so comforting.'

Carly had found a support, whether it be her unconscious that had arranged it, or whether her father 'in spirit' was there to help her, by tapping in to the memory of a loving, supportive father. The important thing was that she should feel all right about it, and not to feel it as yet another stress to worry about. This was the important thing to achieve. By giving her the various explanations, Carly was eventually able to relax and accept it. ('You don't think I'm mad then!').

Are we being cared for, looked out for, by others in another dimension? Do some people have the ability to be aware of this other dimension? Sue Leet, NLP (Neuro Linguistic Programming) therapist and hypnotherapist, says she knows so. Sue says her ability to see, and also to feel and hear, '… gives me a knowledge that when a person or animal passes on, life will continue in some form and I am able to interact with them on a different level.' Sue has helped many people by doing just this, and also experiences herself as a bridge between animals and humans.

Many people's ability to 'see' started in childhood, and very often these children were misunderstood and felt isolated. The following is a story that not only deals with a child's spiritual encounters but also deals with childhood bereavement and is based on the true story of a psychic's early experiences. If you ever know of a child who you feel may get comfort from this story, please read it to them. It is written here on behalf of all children, and also so that we as adults may gain more understanding.

The Special Girl

Once there was a little girl called Tina. She lived with her mummy and daddy in a bungalow with fields all around it, just outside of the town. In the summer the birds sang loudly and sometimes little rabbits came into the garden from the field to play. In the winter the birds would fly down into the garden and eat the bread that Tina would throw down for them, especially in the snow when they really needed it. There was a big old shed in the garden and Tina's dad had cut a hole in the side so the birds could fly in for shelter. Sometimes in the spring there was a nest and then Tina would be very careful when she went into the shed not to disturb the mummy bird, who might be sitting on the eggs until they hatched. Later, Tina would be careful not to disturb the mummy or the daddy bird, busy flying in and out of the hole bringing worms and insects for the baby birds to eat, who were sometimes cheeping very loudly in the nest. 'It's important to be quiet,' said Daddy, 'we don't want to frighten them away!' When Daddy was home at the weekends he would take Tina for long walks over the fields and through the woods, telling her about the birds, plants, and little animals they would often see. When they came back, Mummy always had a cake and a drink ready for her, and Daddy would make him and Mummy a pot of tea. One day, Tina came home from school, getting off the school bus as she always did at the end of the lane, and she saw that Mummy had tears in her eyes. She suddenly felt a very sad feeling and was a little bit scared as she hadn't seen Mummy like this before. Mummy got Tina her usual drink and biscuit, and then sat down and told her that Daddy was in bed and very ill. She said a nurse would come in every day to help look after him. Tina wanted to see Daddy then, and ran down the hall to the bedroom. Daddy had his eyes closed and Mummy said he was sleeping as he was very tired. After that, Daddy had his eyes closed a lot and didn't talk to Tina very much. Mummy had those tears in her eyes a lot as well. Tina was feeling very lonely and worried about Daddy who was ill, and Mummy who was sad.

One day, Tina started to walk down the hall to Daddy's bedroom when she saw the hall was full of people. They were all looking at her and she felt a bit scared. But then a funny thing happened. When Tina kept walking down the hall they didn't move out of the way, but Tina found she could walk right through them! Tina could hear the people were telling her not to be frightened because they were there to help her, so she wouldn't be lonely. Mummy came out of the kitchen to ask Tina if she wanted fish fingers for tea, but the strange thing was that it was obvious Mummy couldn't see the people or hear what they were saying.

When Tina went to bed that night she found all the people waiting for her in the bedroom. She felt comforted as they had told her they were there to help her, and one of them did a funny dance and made her laugh. Another one pulled funny faces. Tina's mother came in to see if she was asleep, and said she must try to go to sleep as she had to be up early for the school bus. When she had gone, Tina realised her mother definitely couldn't see the people. She felt they were special then, and were really just for her, and that made her feel special too. Tina got out of bed and opened the doors to the big cupboard that was in the corner of her bedroom. 'It's time to go to sleep now,' she announced to the people, 'you must all get in the cupboard.' And they did! There was one who popped his head out, grinning at her and cheekily sticking out his tongue, but he soon went back in and all was quiet. Tina called them 'The Funny People'.

One morning, Mummy came in to her bedroom and told Tina that Daddy had died in the night. Mummy had tears again and was very quiet and sad. Tina felt scared, and also very sad as she knew she wouldn't see Daddy again. Mummy was very quiet for the next few days and didn't talk to her hardly at all.

Suddenly, Tina's aunty arrived and said to her, 'You're going to come and stay with me in the town for a little while.' Tina didn't want to go with her aunty, as she was worried about Mummy being sad by herself, but Mummy said it was 'the best thing' and that she could come home again after a few weeks.

When Tina got to her aunty's, she felt even more lonely and sad. She missed Mummy and Daddy, and although her aunty had given Tina toys to play with and things to do, she didn't talk to Tina much.

One day, Tina was sitting on the bed looking out of the

window, feeling very sad and wishing she could go home, when she saw a little boy in the tree outside. It was very strange, as the little boy seemed to kind of peel off the tree and the next thing he was sitting on the bed, right beside her! Not only that but he started to talk to her just like The Funny People did. He wasn't actually speaking out loud but she could hear him in her head. He told Tina his name was Danny and he had come to play with her so she wouldn't be lonely, and Tina told Danny all about her mummy and daddy.

After that Tina didn't feel lonely as she had Danny to play with. One day, her aunty came into her room and said she had heard Tina talking to herself a lot lately. Tina told her about her new friend, Danny. Her aunty told her not to be silly, that there was no little boy there, but Tina knew she was wrong. Every day, Tina played with Danny and started to feel happier. After a while, her aunty told Tina that she was going back home to Mummy. 'Then perhaps you'll get rid of this Danny nonsense,' she said.

Tina was pleased she was going home. When she got back to Mummy, she realised Danny had come with her! He was in the bungalow and ready to play! Later, when Mummy set the table for tea, Tina put out another plate and mug for Danny. 'Why have you set three places?' asked Mummy. 'It's for Danny, my new best friend,' said Tina. 'Look Tina, you've got to stop this nonsense,' said Mummy. 'There's no one else here, only you and me.' 'Well, I can see him!' replied Tina.

Then Mummy did let her keep Danny's place at the table, and he would sit down with them every day for meals. One day, Mummy said, 'You're going to stay with your cousins on their farm for a little while.' Tina thought this might be fun as she loved animals, although she had never met her cousins, nor her aunty and uncle.

When Tina got to the farm, she realised Danny hadn't come with her. Her cousins were very noisy and her uncle seemed to shout a lot. Tina didn't feel she fitted in very well. She would escape down to the stables. One mare had a little foal and Tina would sit stroking the foal and talking to the horses.

There was a dog called Ben, who had come from another home when his owner had died. 'My Daddy died,' she told Ben. 'I know how sad you are.' She felt Ben talked to her, not in words of course, but she would hear little bits of stories when she was with Ben, how he had lived for many years with a lady called Molly, and how happy he had been walking in the park, playing with a ball, and sitting with Molly in the evenings. Tina told Ben all about Daddy and how she missed him – then suddenly the tears came. 'It's good to cry,' said Ben. 'It usually makes me feel a bit better afterwards.' One day, the vet came and said Ben had conjunctivitis, as his eyes were all red. 'He hasn't got conjunctivitis,' said Tina to the vet. 'He's crying 'cos he's sad.'

When Tina eventually went home to Mummy, she found that Danny wasn't there either, but she felt very different now since she had been at the farm with the animals. Of course she would still miss Daddy, but now she was able to enjoy the happy memories of the times she had spent with him.

Tina realised she didn't need Danny anymore or The Funny People and that they must have gone to help another little girl or boy. Mummy was happier now and was talking again. They started to go for walks over the meadows, and one day Mummy came home with a little puppy for Tina. Tina called him Ben.

When Tina grew up, she could still hear stories and messages from animals. She also heard people, too, like The Funny People. Tina found she was able to help people who were sad or in trouble by speaking to animals or by listening to the people that no one else could see. Once she had grown up, she never actually saw them anymore like she had as a child; she only heard them. Tina always said that was because her family kept telling her she couldn't really see them, but she had known she could. She also knew she was special too, so in the end that was all that mattered!

Experiences after bereavement have been recounted to me by many people:

'I keep seeing my husband in the house – it's unsettling, I'm not sure what to do.'

'I felt my wife get into bed beside me, I tell you it freaked me out a bit!'

'I saw my brother at a family wedding, it was like a flash and I thought, there's Jim! Then my daughter saw him too, standing beside the bride and groom. We accepted it and found it comforting.'

'My little dog jumps on to my bed. I know she's there.'

'When I came home my cat would be heard jumping down from a bed where she would sleep, two thuds as she came down. For six or seven weeks after she died, I still heard those thuds. I would wake at night with the feeling my toes were being bitten, and there was the pressure of her lying beside me.'

One theory says this can all be part of the grieving process as the self is struggling to accept the loss, but some of these people said they were not struggling to accept the loss. Others will say it is the spirit of the person or animal being in another dimension, or an imprint of energy left behind.

We know it happens and it is common. The important thing is that it is accepted as normal.

I See Dead People

We are all born with various natural abilities, and I have found invariably people who 'see' as a matter of course through life were born with this ability.

As I came across more and more incidents of paranormal experience within my work, I was coming across these things in my everyday life too. I will share some of these experiences with you in the following pages.

Pete tells a story of his childhood, when he was aware of people 'moving around in his bedroom' as he lay in the bottom bunk. He says this occurred on and off between seven and nine years old and he never told anyone. 'I didn't think I should, I may not have been believed.' The first time he experienced it, he said he felt scared,' and then after that he felt very apprehensive. 'I felt they were aware of me, but they didn't interact with me, and when I touched one on the arm it crumbled away – there was water all over the floor.'

Pete said he would wake in the night and see them. It wasn't until he was in his forties that he mentioned it to his mother. His mother told him the people he saw in his bedroom as a child had been thrown down a well many years ago. How did she know this? It turned out that his mother had abilities to 'see' and hear. It was six years after this revelation that a TV programme was broadcast investigating human remains found in an ancient well site. The conclusion of the investigation was that the human remains were from the bodies of people who had been murdered and thrown down the well in medieval times. The well site was in Norwich, as was Pete's childhood home.

I met Terry when I started my training. We were in the same study group, but it wasn't until we bumped into each other again about fifteen years later and he heard what I was studying that he started to tell me about himself. Terry says there are people walking around without bodies, and some of them don't know they're dead. He senses the presence of others and he also hears them. The people he senses and hears are very close he says, but are not of this earthly world or dimension as he calls it, and are out of reach as earthly individuals. After his mother died, a picture kept coming into his head of her dancing with his father, both of them looking at him and smiling. He tells how his mother and father would dance together when they were very young, before he was born, so he had never actually seen them dance. 'She's happy now,' said Terry. 'I don't need to see her body at the hospital, it's just a husk, it's not her – she is free of that body now and happy, no pain anymore. I can't explain how I know this, I just do.' His experiences are normal for him, although there were problems when his mother was alive as she had difficulty in accepting them. This had resulted in a feeling of trepidation regarding these incidents and who he could tell. As time went by and Terry was able to meet up with like-minded people, he gradually learned to trust himself and gained in confidence. When present at a death he has said on more than one occasion after the person has passed on, 'Keep talking, they can still hear you.'

'I never say my father has died,' says Terry, 'I say he's moved on, as I know he's gone to the next stage. I sense him sometimes, I know he's here.'

When Terry asked me to join the local Ghost Hunters group I was in two minds. 'Ghost Hunters'? It sounded like we were all seven years old again, forming another secret society. What is a ghost anyway? Something scary from a film or a story? Armed with this rather flippant attitude, I accompanied Terry to the pub where they held their monthly meetings. Joining them at the table with my pint of lager shandy, I was introduced to some very friendly and down to earth people who made me feel very welcome. My attitude melted away as I relaxed, put at ease by their humorous yet serious approach. Terry told me the difference between a ghost and a spirit is that the ghost is an 'imprint', an energy left behind from the past in the place where it is being experienced, whereas a spirit is a previous earthly person who has 'moved on', and can be seen or sensed by some including himself, in their next dimension of existence. It was all far from my flippant conclusions. 'Don't expect anything,' said Terry when I agreed to attend the next vigil. 'Sometimes nothing happens.'

My First Investigation

We stood silently in the pitch-blackness of the dungeon, Gordon the ex-curator of the castle (and the spitting image of Doc from *Back to the Future*) inviting any spirits that might happen to be around that night to join us. I had been told that Gordon was very well known to the group, being an extremely spiritual person with lots of experience over the years of working at the castle.

Nothing happened for a while and then the EMF monitor which records electromagnetic energy flashed yellow to orange. 'There's no electricity in the building,' said Gordon. The only lights we had that night were candles. It was mostly a ruin apart from a central structure of two rooms reached by a magnificent flight of wide stone steps, with the dungeon beneath. As the lights on the monitor flashed, Gordon welcomed the spirit, and asked if they were male or female. It was discerned to be male by the flashing lights, and after further questioning by Gordon, one of the mediums said, 'He's saying "pardon", and he keeps repeating it.' 'Are you having trouble understanding me?' Gordon asked the spirit. No response from the lights. 'Are you *asking* for a pardon? Have you been wrongly accused?' asked Gordon. It would seem from the sudden blaze of lights from yellow through orange to red that this must indeed be the case. Suddenly Terry, who is clairsentient, said, 'I'm feeling scared, I'm wringing my hands and I can't stop.' 'Are you frightened?' Norman asked the spirit. Another blaze of lights and the equipment turned off altogether. 'He doesn't trust anyone,' said the medium. 'He's had a bad time, no one cares.' Suddenly I was aware of the man standing next to me who was shivering profusely. 'I'm freezing,' he said. 'It's common,' said Norman. 'It will soon pass.' 'He's frightened and panicky,' continued the medium. 'He says they are coming, he's in despair.' 'Tell us if you would like us to help you,' said Gordon. 'We care about you, and you can trust us.' Gordon now seemed to be affected and was stumbling over his words. We waited in the darkness, the EMF monitor still switched off. 'Give us a sign,' said Gordon. 'Maybe a sound?'

'I see him slumped against the wall,' said the medium. 'Utterly dejected and getting weaker.' We waited in the darkness and then suddenly the machine flashed. 'OK,' said Gordon, 'you would like us to help you. Look for the light, it is white and welcoming.' We waited, and then after some time had passed, the monitor lit up the area as the lights flashed up and down, from yellow through orange to red, back and forth, back and forth went the lights. 'He's found it,' said the medium. 'Go to the light!' exclaimed Gordon. 'Kind hands are reaching out to welcome you and help you through.' The lights continued their colourful dance and then stopped. 'He's smiling,' said the medium. 'He's safe now.'

Gordon was visibly moved by the whole experience and was wiping his eyes. 'He was a nice man,' said Terry. 'He had no one.'

Outside, we walked across the expanse of grass towards the huge castle mound. I saw the sky had cleared and there was a full moon, our long shadows strung out across the grass. We came to a small area, fenced off, with a little flight of steps leading down into a ruin of a chapel. Terry wouldn't go down them. 'It feels wrong, there's something bad.' I took out my camera and flashed away, photographing each area of the chapel as we looked down. Not one shot came out; they were all blank. 'It's a good camera, too!' I said. I didn't feel what Terry felt and went down into the chapel ruin – it was only a few steps and some of the others were already down there. The stone walls ended in a round chancel. I realised Terry had followed me. 'I can't go any further,' he said. 'It's so strong... Something bad happened here.' I went into the chancel and took more photos. The only ones that showed anything were the ones looking out of the chapel towards the tops of the walls. All the photos taken looking down into the chapel and inside the chapel itself were blank.

We explored the stone steps and passageways inside the ruin of the castle. Several people had said they smelled roses. I smelled nothing. Even Gary, a sceptical young man, had smelled the roses. 'It's such a heavy perfume,' said Terry. 'Attar of roses,' said the medium, appearing through the gloom. 'The perfume is very strong, just what they needed to mask the smells of the time.' We continued down the narrow passage and Terry picked up the smell of almonds; this time he was the only one.

'This place has so much activity,' said Terry.

Thinking about the night's events, I liked the gentle, respectful approach of Gordon, asking permission to help, and the eventual healing that had taken place in the dungeon.

Some psychic experiences are reported as dreams. Ellie had psychic dreams from when she was a young girl. These would be about real events and gave her information – sometimes valuable information that could be given to the police. Ellie was disturbed by these dreams; her husband wasn't keen on her talking about it, and discouraged her from sharing her experiences. Ellie eventually experienced a dream where a 'terrible, evil monster' arose from the ground roaring 'Stop! You have not the right!' So terrifying and disturbing was this, Ellie sought help from a therapist who worked with psychic phenomena. The 'terrible monster' was explained as an extension of herself. Years of blocking or trying to block these experiences by ignoring them and denying them, further discouraged by her husband, had eventually caused a phenomena in her dreams to surface, forcibly attempting to stop the process in a monstrous and terrifying way. It was her subconscious or preconscious at work. With the encouragement of the therapist to accept her ability and work with it, sharing it in her daily life, Ellie's dreams became calmer, with no repeat of the awful nightmare.

Clairvoyant, clairsentient, clairaudience, medium – there are many terms to describe the seeing, sensing and hearing abilities that some possess. When these people come together, they find they are talking about the same thing and there is a mutual understanding, where no one needs to explain – it is a shared ability of knowing.

There are some that claim anyone can develop these skills, but that's not my experience. I'm not saying it cannot be done, but being born with it means it is there whether you like it or not, and that is my common experience of the many people I've come into contact with over the years. Sometimes it doesn't emerge until a certain event triggers it, depending on how open we have learned to be. A certain lady I knew would get very annoyed with it. 'Going into the local supermarket and seeing all these dead people – the live ones are enough to cope with!' she would say.

Research has cited how some people's brains are more sensitive than others, and how some people have the ability to see significant electromagnetic energy, and the seers will say 'we know this already'. The book *Seeing Ghosts; Experiences of the Paranormal* by Hilary Evans gives more reading on research.

There does not seem to be any research or explanations about experiences from birth, where events can occur daily in many different environments, not just in supposedly 'haunted houses'.

What is normal? Usually we adopt the view of normal as it applies to the majority of things we know and experience. Is it anything to do with dying? What happens when we die? These answers are constantly being sought. People say they know what happens, governed by their faith. Others say they know what happens governed by their instincts and experiences. Both say they're right, as they feel they're right. The spiritualists say they have proof. 'We can't explain it, we just know.'

Those people born with a sense of 'seeing' – being able to see, sense, and hear things that the majority of others cannot, will say yes, there is evidence, we see it, we hear it, but many others ignore them; some through fear, some through their religion, and some through just not being able to accept what is being said. For many people these psychic experiences are normal, something they have had as far back as they can remember, often a family trait shared and experienced together. But some have not shared. Brought up in families where denial is encouraged or even where aggression and abuse is directed at a child who tries to share what he or she is experiencing, many learn to suppress their experiences, and some live in fear that they are 'going mad'.

The theory of parallel universes, which was the stuff of fantasy and science fiction, is now being accepted by some scientists, even to explain the Big Bang theory as a collision between two of these parallel universes. 'When we go to the other side,' said Terry, 'maybe we enter one of these universes, as after all they are very close to us – perhaps I'm picking up these people from there.'

Are these natural experiences hardwired within us to allay the fear of death? Are they proof of an afterlife? One day we'll find out, as human beings' quest for knowledge continues.

Normality only exists for the person experiencing it. What can be normal for one person may not be normal for another. 'Paranormal' means crossing the boundary of normal experience, but for some people it becomes a paradox – a 'normal paranormal'.

Near Death Experience

Jilly tells us a story of her neighbour and his experience when he goes into hospital for his operation. These experiences, near death experiences (NDEs), are common and have been studied and documented in many cultures. Dr Sam Parnia, a trailblazer in the study of this phenomenon, cites lucid thoughts and memories in a person at a time when there is no brain activity. His books make very interesting reading.

One example of a client of mine with a near death experience was Ann, a mother struggling with a son who had behavioural problems. I am always required to work with a parent wherever possible in these situations, as children's negative behaviour usually demonstrates something negative going on within the family or other environment. The child would be displaying reactive behaviour, and it is my job to find out what's wrong and assist for change. As my relationship built up with Ann, she started to share some of her own childhood experiences. It can help a parent to understand their children if they remember how they felt as children and some of the things they went through. Ann was sixteen when her elder sister was driving her to college and they were involved in a very bad car crash. Ann was in a coma for six weeks and said she can never to this day remember the accident. Her first conscious memory is waking in hospital and remembering a dream. 'There was a bright light – it was like a tunnel. It felt wonderful, so much love. I so wanted to go through this tunnel and I did. My sister was there; she said, "Go back, it's not your time," but I didn't want to, as it all felt so loving.' Ann was so ill, it was three weeks after she came out of the coma that she eventually learned her sister had died in the crash. Ann said she felt her sister was now in another place, and she said she had no fear of death after that. This experience is the same as many others I have heard, the same descriptive words and feelings, the repetition of a third party saying 'It's not your time'. As Jilly's neighbour reported after his NDE, other people I have talked to also say any fear of death has gone. A typical comment has been 'It's like I've seen through to the next stage.'

Out of Body Experience

Another occurrence to be brought to me is the out of body experience (OBE). There are many writings about this in many different settings, but the one which clients have talked to me about has always been one of physical abuse. A client relating a story of themselves as a child in an unbearable environment will frequently relay the experience of watching themselves being abused. 'It was like I came out of my body, I was on the other side of the room, and was watching myself, feeling nothing. Then suddenly I was back there again, in that horrible place.' This situation, reported time and time again, suggests an ability some of us have, or maybe potentially all of us have, to survive unbearable circumstances, a natural defence mechanism when events just get too much to cope with.

Poltergeist

Poltergeist translated means noisy ghost: objects seem to move by themselves or disappear altogether, radios or stereos mysteriously turn themselves on, there are unexplained noises and even disembodied physical attacks; these are all recognised as poltergeist activity.

A typical experience of a poltergeist was brought to me by a young woman as a scary experience of a knife suddenly flying off the kitchen worktop. Studies have linked this type of activity to energy emitted by a person, invariably a young person and one who is angry. The anger is often suppressed and unexpressed, which has proved interesting for me as this has been the case with all the clients I have worked with who have reported a problem of poltergeist activity. Anger can be a huge energy to suppress and carry. There are also people who still believe the activity is caused by a ghost or spirit. Other people have said to me it is caused by residual anger left behind as an energy from the past.

All this information is given to the client, who can make up their own mind about what to believe. They can then start to accept it and understand why, not believing that they are going mad or imagining it all.

The important result for me is that noisy ghost or not, once the anger has been worked with, understood and dissipated, the poltergeist activity has stopped in every case.

Evil

A young man guns down a class of children in a school in America. A terrible, inexplicable tragedy. What could possess someone to commit such a terrible act, we ask ourselves? 'He is evil.' 'Only someone who is truly evil could do something like this.' 'It's the work of the devil.' 'He is possessed.' 'The devil is to be feared.' 'I have made a pact with the devil.'

It can seem amazing that today, some people are still thinking and talking in terms that seem more suited to medieval times. Until the work of Sigmund Freud, when we learned to understand behaviour, people did believe that those with mental disorders were possessed by evil spirits. As we learned about the different causes of behaviour, and were able to understand the reasons, we also learned that people could change behaviour, could think differently and feel differently. Some people are unable to take responsibility for their actions and will shy away from acknowledging their behaviour; they will be unable to change while they are adopting these defences. Sometimes a person is too damaged to be able to engage for help; 'damaged' could mean emotional or physical damage, as in a brain injury.

The words 'possessed by the devil' we can now replace with other terms, for example emotionally disturbed, scarred, damaged, immature, out of control, psychopathic. Psychopathic behaviour constitutes no conscience, an inability to feel or empathise, and can be the result of experience plus personality, or a result of brain structure and damage. If a person is cruelly treated they can learn to shut off their feelings to survive. This can make it difficult to empathise with others. We can use the words 'evil behaviour' if we wish, but humans create it through their weaknesses, their vulnerabilities, their ignorance, their hurts, their anger, and their resulting cruelties.

I was sitting in a lovely garden on a warm summer day, enjoying tea and home-made cake at a local gathering, when the man sitting next to me paused over his buttered scone and proceeded to tell me about a friend of his who was possessed by an evil spirit. The symptoms he described were the same symptoms that are regularly brought to me by people who are suffering from anxiety and depression. As I pointed out some of these facts, I could see how fervently he believed that this entity had a hold over his friend. What would happen if his friend came to me with this entity? I was thinking this even before he finished the story. If someone did what was wanted, which was apparently an exorcism, would this have worked? The answer is possibly 'yes' because the real problem was not that the person was possessed, but that they *believed* they were possessed.

If the belief is replaced with another belief that the entity has gone, then the symptoms could lessen. However, the belief is still present that an entity can invade, so symptoms could recur.

When someone comes to me with symptoms that are recognised as depression and anxiety, we work together to find out when the symptoms started, we discover the reasons for them, and I give tools for the person to work with and rid themselves of the symptoms. Finally the person can go forward with an understanding of the condition, and change their way of life to avoid any repetition in the future. This couldn't happen with beliefs of possession by evil spirits.

Psychosis – The Difference

People who have psychic experiences very often do not tell others or at best, only certain others who they can trust and who maybe share their experiences.

There are people who have a type of psychotic experience that used to be – and still sometimes is – called 'having a breakdown'. They retreat from the real world into their own world, made up of their own experiences.

A friend of mine had a sister who said she saw people regularly in her garden. One day my friend got an urgent phone call: one of these people had started to dig up her vegetable patch. When my friend went to her sister's house there was nothing happening but her sister was insistent. Then there were people in the house, she said, and one person was sitting on her bed. My friend could see there was nothing there. The difference between this experience and many other stories I had heard of 'seeing', was that the sister had no concept that this might not be real to others. She would tell everyone about it and get quite angry if people disagreed with her or tried to tell her it wasn't happening. Eventually, she was so affected by the happenings that she wasn't looking after herself properly and had to go into a mental health unit to be cared for.

There are reasons for a psychosis. Some medical conditions, for example HIV, AIDS, Parkinson's Disease and brain tumour can be a cause, also overdoses of medication, large amounts of alcohol and drugs, or withdrawal from these, can all cause a psychotic episode. If depression is severe, a psychosis can occur. The delusions and hallucinations of schizophrenia, bipolar disorder with its extreme mood swings, and sometimes a severe postnatal depression, can also cause the experience of a psychotic episode. In most cases of psychosis, medication can be given to help the chemical balance in the brain return to normal.

You may have someone close to you who you think is not behaving normally – who has lost touch with reality. It can be very difficult to cope when things have developed to this extent, as the person will very often not believe there is anything wrong with them. Contacting their doctor is the first step to obtaining help.

My mother-in-law suffered a psychosis at one time. My father-in-law had died suddenly; it had been a shock, he had been very fit and active and now suddenly he was dead. I would go and sit with her in her little bungalow and we would chat. She started to say some strange things. 'When I watched *Kilroy* (a television talk show), he came out of the TV and sat there, where you are. We had a good conversation!' She said it like it was true. She didn't say: 'This is going to sound really weird but I thought Kilroy came out of the TV and talked to me.' According to her, this had really happened. My husband would get impatient and tell her not to be silly. 'Of course he didn't, don't be daft.' She would then get very upset and quite angry with him. 'You have to talk to her like you believe it, it's the only way,' I said. I had found this out not by professional knowledge at that time, but by instinct. I felt I understood her world and what she wanted. She got worse and wouldn't go out into the garden because she saw strangers there. Then the house became less secure for her as she thought someone had taken out her lounge window, so she wouldn't go in there. She saw people up the trees and children on the roof. She was given help and was eventually able to recover. We now know there are reasons, usually extreme mental stress, for what used to be known as a 'nervous breakdown' when the mind just cannot seem to cope anymore. Healing time is needed and very often medication, too.

Bipolar depression can manifest in several strengths and forms. One client was a workaholic for years, holding down high-powered demanding jobs, periodically becoming overcome with a complete lack of energy and feeling down, and having to have six months off work. This became a pattern in life – extreme work than a complete retreat from life. The energy pattern of the extreme high and the extreme low. Once she recognised her limits she was able to use her energy in the most healthy way for her, by completely changing her lifestyle. There were no more episodes after that.

A close friend of mine, Sally, suffered a bipolar episode. A bad bereavement on top of many years of pushing herself to the limit and carrying feelings of guilt and low self-esteem resulted in Sally feeling very 'down' and having no energy. She was living with a kind friend who had offered a place to stay. It became stressful for the friend however as suddenly Sally found she was wide-awake at night and started wandering around the house. This could last for many nights. Eventually not knowing night from day, Sally would be making breakfast at 3 a.m. thinking she was being helpful. Eventually, the friend contacted the doctor and Sally was referred to the mental health unit. I visited her several times and we often had quite normal, enjoyable conversations – but suddenly something would be said and I realised that all was not right. 'Look at all these people in here,' she said to me one day. 'I'm going to be the one who cures them all,' and 'You see that tree over there, I sit under it and the tree tells me these things.' It was no good arguing with her or putting reasoning in place. That was how it was according to Sally and she believed it. This is the difference between psychotic and psychic. With a psychic experience there is awareness of the whole picture, but with a psychotic experience there is just one picture: their subjective experience. According to them, what they're saying is true and that is without doubt what is happening, so everyone should be able to see it, or at least believe them.

When she was well again, Sally didn't remember most of what she'd said, but she did remember making the breakfast in the night and remembered genuinely feeling she was helping.

Sally was given medication to help her mind. She was given rest, both mental and physical, to recharge her batteries. She was given therapy to deal with some of her past issues. She was given information as to what her triggers were and how she needed to conduct her life in the future to avoid another episode.

Today she is still on medication, many people do need to take medication for the rest of their lives, but she is leading a normal, happy life with a boyfriend and running a business, doing what she enjoys. She has learned to recognise when she is overdoing it, she knows the signs and with the help of the medication is able to control the bipolar tendencies.

I had been working with Jane for many months. We had dealt with a bullied childhood, being bullied at work, an unhappy marriage, an unhappy affair, and then her mother who she was very close to died.

We were doing our session as normal and she had been talking about her mother when she suddenly said, 'You know John Taylor, the bass guitarist with Duran Duran? Well, I'm going to marry him!'

Had she managed to meet John Taylor in this country backwater where she lived? Had their eyes met across the room in the local Dog and Duck? Maybe. On further questioning sadly this was not the case. 'I just know I am, it's definitely going to happen.' She was not even seeing it as strange, or impossible, or highly unlikely, as John Taylor was probably around thirty-five then and she was fast approaching fifty; I know age is no barrier but it just seemed all things considered completely delusional. And it was. Jane's husband took her to the doctor, and she was able to receive treatment from the mental health team. Jane was diagnosed as experiencing an episode of bipolar depression, from which she eventually recovered, after a time in the mental health unit; a time of rest and medication. When she finally recovered she still had to take her medication, but she resumed her professional life and was more emotionally and mentally equipped than before.

Those people unfortunate enough to have a psychosis commonly truly believe their phenomenon is the real world and when challenged can sometimes become quite angry and aggressive. Often they don't seem to understand or acknowledge what is being said to them. People who have seeing and sensing experiences, like my client Sarah, experiencing seeing a woman all her life that others could not see, and the carpet fitter in Jilly's house seeing someone standing by the stairs, are very aware that their experience is not what the majority see, and know they may be regarded as not normal, or worse, mad, so they are careful with whom they share their stories. They are living their day-to-day lives in a healthy way.

Those with psychosis are not aware and can find problems with everyday living start to escalate. Those not in a psychosis, but having a paranormal experience, have an awareness and are living their lives as others are.

Psychosis is usually easy to recognise as things the person is saying and the way they are saying them just won't seem right. If you are not sure then checking it out with them will confirm it.

Listening Is So Important

When listening to people's stories as a therapist, the important thing is to listen actively. Listening actively? Do you dance around the room when you do it then? Ha ha to the friend who said that, but it is surprising how many people listen and don't actually truly hear what the person is saying.

A simple example of not listening actively is the story of a trainee counsellor working within an organisation who had a complaint made against her. The client had told the counsellor she had never got on with her mother, who never had time to see her and didn't seem to care about the grandchildren or indeed herself. Her experience of childhood had been one of feeling neglected and unwanted.

The trainee had replied, 'Oh well, I expect she was busy.' Immediately, the client felt she was not being listened to or understood.

Active listening means understanding from the words how the client feels and how he or she sees the situation. In this case, it is neglected and abandoned, a feeling which goes right back to early childhood. Making non-evidence based reasons for the mother's behaviour in this instance is not going to give the client a feeling of someone who understands or is listening. Listening actively means we can respond in ways that show we understand what the client is actually saying; we are hearing how she feels. 'It sounds like it's been very hard for you,' or 'That must have been tough,' would be more appropriate responses as we listen to and feel for this person. Now we are 'with' the client, and ready to explore ways forward for the client, to hear her story and to work through with her, discharging her feelings about her mother, maybe eventually finding what she needs elsewhere, to develop other relationships that are healthy and supportive, or maybe there is a way through with her mother.

Active listening in our relationships can bring us closer together.

I hope you have enjoyed reading the stories in this book, I know I enjoyed working with each case that has been included. The childhood stories are all generally happy stories of happy childhoods. Many clients who come to me with life problems will say, 'Oh no, my childhood was a happy one!' And it was, but when we start to 'take it apart' and look at small incidents, they tell an extra story that can answer questions and help to solve present problems. Maybe you too will benefit from some of the information here, as you go through your own life story. 'But what about Jilly's children?' 'Did the girls have nice boyfriends?' 'What happened to Tom?' 'What did Jilly do after Annie's reading, what was she born to do?' Ah! Now you know what it's like to be a therapist!

'Clinical diagnoses are important since they give ... a certain orientation, but they do not help the patient. The crucial thing is the story for it alone shows the human background and suffering, and only at that point can the therapy begin to operate.'
Carl Jung, psychiatrist 1875–1961.